T0160802

PERCEPTION
SEEING IS NOT BELIEVING

PERCEPTION
SEEING IS NOT BELIEVING

**IT'S TIME
TO EVOLVE**

JAMES & STEPH PURPURA

Waterside Productions

Printed in the United States of America
First Printing, 2019

ISBN-13: 978-1-941768-27-3 print edition
ISBN-13: 978-1-941768-28-0 e-book edition
ISBN-13: 978-1-941768-36-5 audio edition

Waterside Productions
2055 Oxford Avenue
Cardiff, CA 92007
www.waterside.com

CONTENTS

PART FIVE: EMERGING FROM FOG: THE REAL JOURNEY BEGINS

PART SIX: THE ONLY WAY OUT IS THROUGH . . . HELPING OTHERS

PART ONE

ROCK BOTTOM

PERSONAL HELL

THE CRASH: PLAYING THE ENDGAME

Her boyfriend is in the bathroom getting ready for work. He looks up at the reflection in the mirror and sees his girlfriend sleeping in the bed. What he fails to realize is that she is only pretending to be asleep. He is still agonizing about the fight they had the previous week and he glares at her, debating whether or not to wake her up. He looks down at his watch and realizes that if he does, he will be late for work. He shakes his head and storms out of the house.

She doesn't move yet, but when she hears his car door open and close, and hears him pull out of the driveway, she jumps out of bed and runs to the window to make sure he really left. She waits a couple of minutes and starts packing up all her belongings. She looks down at the bruises on her body and says to herself, *What an asshole. I am done letting men treat me this way.*

She packs up her car as fast as she can, jumps in, and speeds away. She feels a sense of desperate urgency in everything she is doing. Six hundred dollars. This is all the money she has to her name. She drives down the highway out of town and keeps going for several hours. The whole time she is berating herself and second-guessing her decisions. The entire drive she thinks about all the other shitty men she has been with. She feels angry and betrayed. She thinks about the fact that her own dad abandoned her after her parents' divorce, and that he doesn't love her, either. She looks in the rearview mirror and says out loud, *I hate you.* She doesn't believe there is anyone in the world who cares about her or who loves her. She feels totally alone.

After several hundred miles, she sees a small dusty desert town up ahead. She pulls off the highway and stops at a local store. She wanders the isles as a debate rages in her head. *What am I going to do? Where am I going to go?* She grabs several items and throws them into her cart. At the cash register she unloads some food, brand-new makeup, hair dye, and a large rope. She doesn't make eye contact with the cashier, who is attempting to make small talk.

She drives to a nearby hotel and checks into a room. As she unloads her car, she starts berating herself again. *Nobody loves you. You have no purpose here. Your life is never going to get better.* She sits down on the hotel bed, dumps out the groceries, and begins pondering the purpose of her life. She picks up the hair dye kit, walks into the bathroom, mixes it all up, and sets it on the counter. She slumps back down on the bed and promptly falls asleep.

The next morning, she wakes up, goes into the bathroom, and sees that the hair bleach has exploded all over the counter. She shakes her head, thinking, *I can't do anything right.* She sits back down on the bed, and there she rests, for hours, ruminating about what to do.

Eventually she grabs a piece of paper and pen off the nightstand and draws a line down the middle of the page. On one side she writes, "Reasons to Live." On the other side she writes, "Reasons to Die." *I feel so alone. I hate myself. My life sucks. My father abandoned me, which means I am unlovable. Nobody gives a shit about me or would miss me. Nobody is going to care or come to my funeral. It will be as if I never existed. I am so tired of feeling alone and unloved.*

Feeling agonizingly sad and depressed, she drops the pen and paper, picks up the rope, and walks into the bathroom. She is numb as she ties one end to the shower head and loops the other end around her neck. She turns on the water and lets it gush over her face. She drops, and the rope jerks tight around her neck. Darkness closes in and all awareness fades to black.

She can feel herself dying, nothing but darkness.

THE CRASH: NO WAY OUT

It's a humid night and a man walks along the beach as he has done every night for the last few months. He looks down at his arms and sees fading track marks from his struggles with addiction, something he's tried repeatedly to overcome. He is replaying the video over and over in his head about how bad his life has become.

Just three months earlier, he was living out west, addicted to just about every drug imaginable. He passed bad checks to support his habit. Drug dealers were looking for him because he owed them money. He was wanted by the police because of all the fraudulent checks he had written. One detective in particular was hell-bent on seeing him pay dearly. A few months before, he had been sitting in a jail cell when the detective showed up and temporarily checked him out of jail into his custody. The cop told him, "I'm working the biggest case of my life and I need you to find somebody for me. You don't know the guy, but he runs in your same drug circles."

He promised the detective that he would do as requested. The detective strapped a tracker to the man and dropped him off at a drug house the man frequented. He walked through the front door, went out the back door, cut off the tracker, and fled the state. He knew he had to get out, otherwise he was going to die. The detective never saw him again.

He made his way to South Carolina and showed up at the front door of a friend of his from high school. He said that he was in trouble and needed help. His friend took him in and helped him get sober. They rented a house together at the beach and the man began to rebuild his life. He changed his identity and tried to live normally. But the nightmare of his past would come flooding in during every walk he took on the beach after work. He would sit on the shoreline and imagine his inner demons swimming off into the ocean.

On this night he walks back to his house, feeling tired from working a double shift at a restaurant. He falls asleep, only to be awakened the next morning by a loud knocking on the door. He opens it and is confronted by a pair of federal marshals who are there to arrest him. He thanks his friend as he says good-bye: "I wouldn't be alive without you. No matter what happens to me, I needed to recover before facing the consequences." The friend gives him a hug and says, "I love you."

And so begins the man's long journey back to his home state on an airplane full of prisoners flying cross-country. When he arrives, a bus takes him to a jail and when the door opens, standing there waiting for him is a guard.

"You're a piece of shit," says the guard. "We were going to catch you eventually. Let's go."

It is a long walk down the hallway, and every step of the way the guard keeps berating him. "You're always going to be a piece-of-shit loser. You'll die with a needle in your arm, or in a prison cell. Once a drug addict, always a drug addict."

The man looks up and protests, "No, no. I'm clean!" The guard laughs and snaps, "Shut up, dumbass, I don't give a fuck what you are. Because you ran, we've arranged for you to be put in the worst part of the jail. What we call our super-max section, reserved for drug kingpins and killers. It's a solitary confinement unit and you're only getting out of your cell one hour every other day, you son of a bitch."

They walk the man to a cell, unshackle his feet, and shove him in. They release the latch to a small opening in the door and order the man to thrust his hands through the hole so they can remove his cuffs. The deafening noise of the cell door slamming is one the man will never forget. As the guard walks away laughing, he shouts one last insult: "You know the best part, asshole, is you haven't been to trial, there is no bail, and you have no idea how long you will be in here!"

The man curls up on the bed and descends into a deep depression.

CHAPTER
2

TAKE A JOURNEY WITH US

THIS IS US

The stories you just finished reading are our stories. The woman in the bed was Steph, and the man getting thrown in the cell was James. These are our deepest, darkest secrets, and we have been running away from them our whole lives. You must be wondering why we are sharing them now. The truth is, we don't want all our suffering to go to waste. If our story can help you grow in your own life, then it will make all the pain we experienced worth it.

We have been on an unbelievable journey that has taken us through hell, and we have risen to a level of success we never dreamed possible. In sharing our experiences we hope you will see some of your story in ours and you will understand that even in the darkest of times, you are not alone. There is hope. That is the reason why we wrote this book.

We will share with you the events leading up to our crash, the climb out of our personal hell, and what it took for us to rise to the top, both personally and financially.

It is our hope that you can rapidly learn the concepts and ideas that it took us fifteen years to fully understand. We will provide you with a road map to get you back to the unique, authentic version of yourself that is waiting to be uncovered.

As you embark on this journey with us, we wish we could tell you that our ascent to the top was all amazing. It had its moments for sure, but most of it was very painful. When we started our life together, we kind of knew what we wanted, but we had no idea how to get it. We decided to figure out how to re-create ourselves and build an amazing life together. That's where the pain came in. We had no clue what we were doing, so everything came out of blood, sweat, and tears. We made many mistakes along the way and hit more dead ends than you can possibly imagine.

As you progress on your journey of personal evolution, we hope you can avoid some of the pain and suffering it took for us to get here. Notice we said some. Nobody gets this sort of transformation without getting knocked down and bruised a few times.

Before we get start, we want to pose a question for you to think about as you take this journey with us.

Do you know what gives your life meaning?

We don't mean your purpose or experiences. We are asking from a purely functional standpoint. You're probably thinking, "Well I guess I have never really thought about that." It's time to start, because we are going to take you on a journey to explore that very question.

There is a tremendous amount of power that comes from knowing and fully understanding the answer to that question. There are two things that dictate your life experience. Everyone knows what they are, yet few of us seem to fully understand how they work. They are perception and emotions.

Perception and emotions not only dictate all your experiences, from beginning to end, but they also give your life meaning. Everything you are, everything you see, everything you experience, is determined by perception. And it is your emotions that give your life the only meaning it has.

As a matter of fact, the only reason you ever do anything is to achieve the emotion you believe will be created by an action or experience. Emotions are truly the only motivation we have in life. These two things are at the core of what it means to be alive. Doesn't it seem odd that most of us don't fully understand perception and emotions? Understanding these concepts and how they work will dramatically improve your life. Have you ever had an experience or emotion that did not make sense to you? Now, for the first time, you are going to know why.

This book is not meant to be a personal development book; it is meant to create a fundamental shift inside you by redefining the way you think about all your experiences, and reshaping how you experience your life. It doesn't matter where you are currently in your life, whether you are at the top of your field, just getting started, or somewhere in between. This book will challenge you on a very deep level. If you take the time to fully understand the concepts and apply them to your life, you will achieve a level of self-mastery you never dreamed possible. It is time to rise up and experience your life to the fullest. It is time to evolve.

WHERE DO WE GO FROM HERE?

Coming out of our experiences we both firmly believed our lives did not make sense. It always felt like life was happening to us, not because of us. We felt very much like a feather blowing endlessly around in the wind.

What we would later discover is that everybody is on a path to somewhere. Our paths brought us to these very tragic points. But the question we were left with was why? Why did we end up in these desperate situations? What was the cause?

Those were the questions we wanted to answer for ourselves, because regardless of how we got there, we didn't want to end up back there again. We understood that there was no way that either of us could survive another fight with darkness. We desperately wanted to make sense of it all. That's where our journey started: with a question.

We made a pact with each other that we were going to rebuild our lives. We had lived lives full of fear, frustration, and disappointment. We each accepted responsibility for the lives we had created, even if we did not fully understand how we had done it. But we believed that if we owned it, that meant we could change it. We set out on a journey to find out how life works, so that we could figure out a way to consciously create a new life for ourselves.

We started looking for books and information that would show us how to create the life of our dreams and stop living out the nightmares of our past. At that time everyone was talking about "the law of attraction." We jumped in with both feet, by watching the movie, and reading all the books we could on the subject. Then we started asking people to describe how it worked. They said it was a secret, and all about bringing up your vibration. What did that mean? You have to come into vibrational alignment with the things you desire. Great, how do we do that? Oh, you get a poster board, you tape pictures of all the things you want on it, then, every day, you just sit and stare at the board and meditate until you come into alignment with it? When do you know when you're in alignment? Well, when you get the stuff you want, of course. How does that really happen? It works on the quantum level, it's about physics and string theory. None of the people we were talking to were scientists, and they were talking about concepts like string theory.

We are not making an argument about whether the law of attraction is real or not. The problem we were having was that this concept kept the power to change our lives out of our control. It felt like we were meditating and waiting for some magical force to bring us the things we desired. We wanted to know how it works, because otherwise it's impossible to duplicate.

We needed something to get to the core of our issues and evoke the real change we wanted in our lives but had not been able to find. We needed something based on facts that told us how things really worked. We wanted to go beyond the old-school self-help books, such as *Think and Grow Rich*, which says things like "Whatever the mind can conceive and believe, it can achieve" and "Thoughts are things." We wanted to know how and why thoughts become things. If we could not understand the underlying process, we were never going to be able to consciously create our lives.

That is when we decided that we would embark on a quest to discover the process for ourselves. We set out to rebuild our lives from the ground up, which was not hard because we were already at the bottom.

We started by working to feel better about ourselves. We both had low self-esteem, so we decided to try improving that. Of course, that is easier said than done. But we were determined and kept trying. We will explain later the process we used, but for now, just know that this is the wrong way. We discovered, however, that sometimes when you go the wrong way, you inadvertently find the right way at some point on the ride.

Our process started something like this. We asked ourselves the question, "What is self-esteem?" Our thought was that it is the opinion we have of ourselves. Okay, if it is our opinion of ourselves, we should just change our opinion. That is where we started. We hated ourselves, so we just started telling ourselves that we loved ourselves. It turned out to be a very difficult process. Even though we told ourselves over and over and over again how we loved ourselves, we did not believe it. But after a while, it did seem like less of a lie.

It felt like we were making progress, so we kept going a little deeper to challenge other beliefs. We added to the list other affirmations, such as: "I am smart." "I am pretty." "I am good enough." We literally followed this process for years. Along the way, a couple of things happened. The first one was shocking: after a long while, our lives started to improve. Then as things started moving along, we started adopting other beliefs. A big one was: "Everything happens in our best interest." We told ourselves that over and over and over again. Hey, guess what? Things started working out for us, and we were like, *Holy shit, this really is working!*

There was, however, one inherent problem with what we were doing. Inserting new beliefs into our subconscious minds did not mean the old beliefs that made up our self-esteem disappeared. The old beliefs faded in the background, but we began to feel like Jekyll and Hyde, living two different lives. We would be moving along great, and seem to be growing, then something would trigger one of these old beliefs and it would feel like we were right back where we started.

Success for us was not about happiness. It was not about getting rid of the darkness; it was about learning how to manage it. The better we got at this process, the faster our lives started to improve. Soon it seemed like there wasn't anything we couldn't create. People around us looked at how fast our lives were growing and were blown away by our progress, and we felt pretty good about it, too. The issue was we had this belief that at some point we would shove the darkness so far down that it would never resurface again. But that never happened. It was always there with us, every step of the way.

It took us many years to put enough positive layers on top of the negative for it to start showing up in our lives. But once it did start showing up, it started growing, and it was mind-boggling how fast things moved along. While we knew the process and could duplicate it and even teach others how to do it, most people did not have the stomach or the motivation for a battle that takes that long. Most everybody we told ended up failing to duplicate our results.

At that point, we stopped, turned around, and tried to figure out the reason why what we were doing was working for us. We spent a long time examining our experiences. It was then that we realized it was all about perception. As we started examining our lives and the role perception was playing, we understood why we were successful. We also understood why most people aren't living up to their potential. The more we dug in, the more we understood which beliefs were affecting us the most and how to enhance those beliefs.

In the chapters that follow, you will find the principles we discovered that will give you the ability to create anything your heart desires. We will show you which principles and beliefs you need to adopt in order to *consciously* create your life. But please understand: there is much more to the story.

We arrived at a point where the darkness was more manageable, but it wasn't gone. We went to work again on how to eliminate the darkness we felt inside. Thank goodness this process didn't take nearly as long as the previous process because we went into it with a fundamental understanding of perception. It turns out that consciously creating your outside world and eliminating the darkness inside are just both sides of the same coin we call perception. We will give you the tools you need to shift your internal perceptions as well.

In this book we discuss many complicated concepts. We are not professors or scientists, but the principles you find in this book are backed by science. We make no claims that we got it exactly right. In the attempt to explain these concepts in a very simple manner, we may have inadvertently transposed some of the words in a way that would make nuances technically incorrect. We worked hard to make the underlying concepts congruent with their scientific meanings. If you want to understand perception at a much deeper level, please refer to a book called *Deviate*, by our personal friend Beau Lotto. Beau is a neuroscientist and one of the world's foremost authorities on the subject of perception.

INTERNALIZE VS. EXTERNALIZE

Did you know that some people internalize their thoughts, feelings, and emotions, while others externalize theirs?

As you read about the events of our lives and how they unfolded, you will recognize a clear pattern. James externalized all his emotions and blamed everything on the outside world. He literally felt like a victim of circumstance and like everyone was out to get him. Steph, on the other hand, internalized all her emotions and blamed everything that went wrong in her life on herself.

This is a very important distinction and one you should look for in yourself. One is not necessarily better than the other, but the internalizing side of the coin can go darker much faster. Prisons are full of people who externalize their emotions and blame the world for all their woes. This is how they justify to themselves all the hate and damage they are inflicting on the outside world. Mental facilities and morgues are full of the people, and the victims of people, who internalize their emotions. Drug rehabs are full of both. Blame is an ugly and dangerous thing that can eat at the minds and hearts of good people.

Along our journey, we've lost a couple of really good friends. Jeff we lost to drug addiction, Tom we lost to suicide from mental illness. One was a victim of externalizing and the other of internalizing. We want to be very clear we are not doctors, therapists, or mental health care specialists. The concepts and ideas in this book are not meant to be a treatment for mental illness. As you continue reading, if you see the darkness in yourself reflected in the darkest parts of our story, we ask that you share your feelings with others and be open to getting professional help if needed.

It is important for you to understand that perception is the source of your internal and external experience. There are some very good professional psychology-based therapies that focus on shifting your internal perceptions. A few we recommend are cognitive behavioral therapy (CBT), eye movement desensitization and reprocessing (EMDR), and somatic psychology. There is no shame in seeking professional help. It will also jumpstart this process by giving you a solid place to begin implementing the ideas in this book. Please seek the help you need, because we do not want to lose any more friends.

FROM NEVERLAND TO THE MATRIX

We all share the same journey. Life starts out for all of us in our own version of Neverland, our younger days filled with wonder and awe. When we suffer our first major rejection, that bubble bursts and we fall into the Matrix, a world that feels forced upon us.

Nothing seems to make sense, and we are left with only two choices; either accept this as a new normal or find a way to climb out. Some of us give up, while others try to climb out and continue to fall. Only a few manage to break free of the Matrix.

We believe that, with the right tools and information, anyone can break free of the Matrix. This book will take you on that journey, the modern-day *hero's journey*.

We have included a description of the different stages, as well as a graph, describing this journey.

Neverland—life as you perceive it as a child, from the vantage point of your unique and authentic self; an inner world of fantasy, imagination, creativity, and the feeling that anything is possible.

The Fall—when we experience major rejection and the bubble of childhood innocence bursts, and with it goes the safety of childhood; you realize that things aren't as you thought they were or should be.

The Matrix—where you land after the Fall. This new world feels like it has been forced on you; you must adapt to cold harsh realities.

The Climb—You begin the escape from the self-limiting confines of the Matrix, attempting to consciously create life circumstances of your own choosing.

The Modern Day Heros' Journey
A Journey into Your Perception

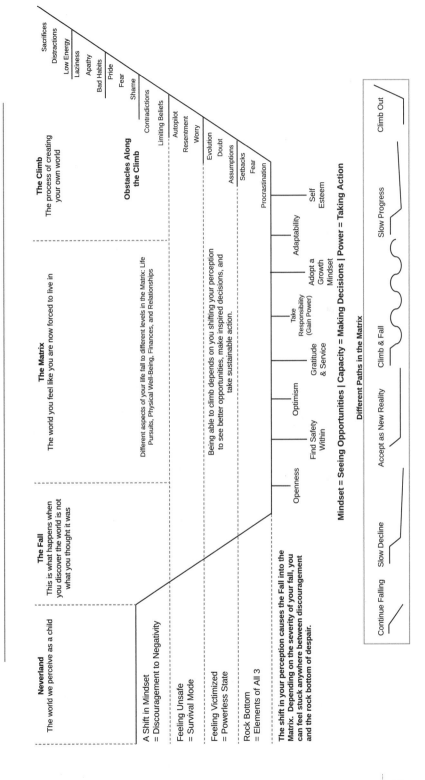

Neverland
The world we perceive as a child

The Fall
This is what happens when you discover the world is not what you thought it was

The Matrix
The world you feel like you are now forced to live in

The Climb
The process of creating your own world

A Shift in Mindset
= Discouragement to Negativity

Feeling Unsafe
= Survival Mode

Feeling Victimized
= Powerless State

Rock Bottom
= Elements of All 3

The shift in your perception causes the Fall into the Matrix. Depending on the severity of your fall, you can feel stuck anywhere between discouragement and the rock bottom of despair.

Different aspects of your life fall to different levels in the Matrix: Life Pursuits, Physical Well-Being, Finances, and Relationships

Being able to climb depends on you shifting your perception to see better opportunities, make inspired decisions, and take sustainable action.

Obstacles Along the Climb

Sacrifices
Distractions
Low Energy
Laziness
Apathy
Bad Habits
Pride
Fear
Shame
Contradictions
Limiting Beliefs
Autopilot
Resentment
Worry
Evolution
Doubt
Assumptions
Setbacks
Fear
Procrastination

Openness
Find Safety Within
Optimism
Gratitude & Service
Take Responsibility (Gain Power)
Adopt a Growth Mindset
Adaptability
Self Esteem

Mindset = Seeing Opportunities | Capacity = Making Decisions | Power = Taking Action

Different Paths in the Matrix

Continue Falling   Slow Decline   Accept as New Reality   Climb & Fall   Slow Progress   Climb Out

IT'S ALL ABOUT U

A DAY IN THE LIFE

As you wake up and start your day, you probably work very hard to stay positive and to keep yesterday's worries from creeping into your mind. Sometimes it works, sometimes it doesn't.

One thing is clear, life is a fight. If you want to succeed and thrive in this world, it's going to take everything you've got. Sometimes the battle seems worth fighting, other times it just doesn't. You look around and you feel like nobody gets it, nobody understands how hard this is, but some of the people around you are fighting their own battles, while others gave up a long time ago.

You often feel alone, even in a room full of people. At some point, maybe something triggers a memory for you that summons feelings of darkness. You start reviewing all the mistakes you've made throughout your life and beating yourself up. Some days you win this battle, other days you don't. Sometimes it lasts for a few minutes, other times for hours.

Often people have good intentions and hearts. They try to understand you, but somehow they seem to miss the mark. At some point in the conversation, they make it about themselves. When you try to express yourself, truly express yourself and let somebody see who you really are, it never seems to work. It always ends up in a misunderstanding.

You can't say for sure whose fault it is. It is better to just keep your mouth shut, and not express your true feelings. It's not that nobody cares, it's just that they have their own shit to deal with, so why would you continue to burden them with your problems? It doesn't seem to do any good anyway.

You want someone to understand you and to tell you you're not crazy. Someone to make you feel better and to let you know everything is going to be okay. This never seems to work, and you just keep fighting, occasionally dipping into negative patterns and behaviors to indulge a little, or sometimes a lot. Of course, this only gives you temporary relief, and then you beat yourself up again for slipping.

Sometimes you might get glimpses of hope; you might actually be winning and changing. You take great pride in the victories, big and small, when they come. The small moments of happiness and joy seem to make the fight all worth it, but this is fleeting because you realize the long-lasting happiness you dream of does not seem to exist.

Some days are more difficult than others, but it is never easy. True happiness feels unattainable, so you hope that tomorrow you will be able to spend more time with the ones who seem to get you on some level, or maybe you can do a few things that give you joy.

At the end of the day, you look back and examine your progress. You sometimes question if it is all worth it. If you are lucky, you get to connect with the people you are closest with, those you can share your ups and downs with, reveal your successes together, and mourn your losses. Your head hits the pillow and you try to drown out the noise, hoping to grab a few hours of sleep to prepare you for the battle that starts again tomorrow.

I SEE YOU

You choose to believe that nobody understands you or your life or how hard your journey has been. In some ways that is true, because nobody has lived your life, walked in your shoes, or fought your battles. In other ways it is not true, because we all have a story and have things in our past we are not proud of.

We want you to know we understand you, what you are going through, and how you feel inside. We want you to know you are not alone. There is nothing wrong with you and there is nothing missing inside you. You are not crazy to feel the way you do. You are not emotionally unstable or damaged in any way.

Everyone has problems, just like you. Some people are just too scared to talk about them. We are happy to reassure you that life does not have to continue to be a fight or a struggle. There is hope, even in the darkest of times. We also need you to understand that you are good enough and smart enough today, just the way you are. Believe it or not, you currently have everything you need to be successful and to feel truly happy and fulfilled. We are going to prove to you that it's time to stop beating yourself up.

What if we told you that you have never made a bad decision? Would that sound strange to you? Would you believe us? What if we said you were fully justified in all your actions and behaviors because you were always doing your best, even when you often did and thought things that were against your own and others' best interests? Yes, you often fall short of your potential, but we still say you have never made a bad decision.

What if we also told you that nothing that has ever happened to you is your fault, but also told you that your outcomes are 100 percent your responsibility? What if we told you that not only have you never made a bad decision, but you're not actually capable of making bad decisions unless you're a sociopath or mentally ill?

Consider: If it is true that you have never made a bad decision, what would this mean to you and your life?

We often look back and second-guess or beat ourselves up for opportunities we missed, decisions we botched, and times we quit or fell short. The voice in your head may be saying, *How could I be so stupid?* or *Why do I keep making the same mistakes over and over?* It's time to stop beating yourself up, because in reality, you're just doing the best you can.

You are probably saying to yourself, okay, this sounds great, but it's hard to believe, because I feel like I have made bad decisions. We will let you off the hook and explain. If your life has not gone the way you wanted or expected, it was because you made decisions using bad information. You might be wondering, okay, what is the difference? It seems like it's only semantics. Actually, it's a big difference, and understanding the difference can set you free.

If your life is not what you want it to be, it's not because you have done anything wrong, it's because you made the only decisions you could with the information you had available to you at the time. You have probably never started a decision-making process by saying, "I think I will do something today that is not in my best interest." To be clear, always doing the best you can on any given day is not the same as living up to your potential.

We all make decisions the same way. Our minds look at all the available information and draw conclusions about the best path forward. We never intentionally set out to make decisions that will harm us. In that moment when we make a decision, we believe it is in our best interest, even if it doesn't turn out that way.

This is why it's so important to understand the difference. While you may have blamed yourself in the past whenever things went wrong, the problem was never you. The problem was the information you used to define your life and make your decisions. Which means . . . there is nothing wrong with you!

You can stop beating yourself up now, because it's a waste of time and you're only doing more damage. You are trying to fix yourself, but you were never the problem in the first place. Your biggest failure has been not taking the time to understand the sources of the information you've used to define your world.

You know at your core that what we are saying is true, yet your mind doubts its validity. This is because you are comparing your results with those of others, or even to your own, based on a different day in your life or on different circumstances.

We are not better than you, nor are you better than us. We have all just had different life experiences, which gave us a different pool of information to access when we make our decisions—that's all. Success and failure in life comes down to information. When you have good information to make decisions, you succeed. If you consider what you have been through, everything about your life makes perfect sense. There is a reason behind every decision you have made and every action you have taken. Every thought, every feeling, every action, every reaction, every fear, every joy had a source.

Let us explain how we discovered this. We have an agreement that we never allow each other to remain in delusion or fear. Which means we always call each other out on everything, all the time, no matter how uncomfortable or chaotic that can be. For a long time, because

James is not a very emotional person, when Steph came to him with a fear-based problem, he would attempt to attack the false belief, and he inadvertently invalidated her emotions and her decision to feel that way in the process.

In James's attempt to help Steph overcome her fears, he totally invalidated her by not recognizing that she made the best decision she could with the information she had available to her, and this made the fears underneath worse because he reinforced the idea that the problem was her and not the information she relied on to make her decision. The fear Steph was using to make her decision was real to her, and she was making the right decision with the information she had available to her at the time.

We realized moving forward that when Steph came to James with a problem, he could validate her decision and the emotions attached to that decision and make her understand that she was not in fact wrong to feel that way. This allowed him to show compassion and understanding when addressing the source of those feelings, which of course was the fear. That proved to be a huge turning point in both our lives and in our relationship.

If you believe us up to this point, you are most likely feeling a little lighter right now. But you are still probably thinking: Okay, if that is true, what is the source of the information and how do I change it? That's a great question and it's the one we intend to answer in the rest of this book.

WHAT LIES BENEATH

Have you ever stopped and wondered, What is my biggest fear? That's a question we have asked ourselves many times over the years. It is a hard one to answer because we do not understand what is going on in our subconscious mind. Not to mention that how we evolved as a species has a lot to do with our fears as well.

It took us years and years, but we can finally say with great confidence that we do know and understand one of the biggest sources of our fears. We know this sounds like a big statement, but give us a couple of pages to prove it to you.

Let's start with this question: Which of the following seems scariest to you?

1. Potential death

2. Instant/certain death

3. Knowing you're going to die in a very short period of time, but you don't know how, you don't know when, and it's most likely going to be excruciatingly painful.

Unless you are a masochist, it is probably safe to assume that number three is the scariest for all of us. You may not be afraid of the concept of death or what happens after you die, but everyone is afraid of dying. The three death scenarios mentioned above correlate with three things we evolved to fear and that are part of our genetic makeup. They came baked into us, which means we do not have a choice. They exist inside us whether we like it or not, and whether we are aware of it or not.

These fears stay dormant in your system until something in your life triggers them and makes them real for you. They keep running until you recognize them and overcome them in some manner.

1. Potential Death

Let's start with the first one, fear of potential death, which is simply the fear of uncertainty. The only reason most people attempt to change is when the fear of not changing becomes greater than the fear of changing. In other words, they only change when they are forced into it, when they feel have no other choice. The fear of uncertainty rose out of our fight for survival, so our belief is to not venture into uncharted territory unless our life depends on it. Period! This fear has always been at the core of who we are, as we evolved not to take chances, not to go outside our comfort zone.

How strong is the fear of uncertainty as a motivator not to change? It's so strong that not even the prospect of certain death is scary enough to get most people to change. You must be thinking, *Wow, that seems like an exaggeration.* But consider this statistic: 90 percent of people who have had coronary bypass surgery fail to change their lifestyle habits, even though they have just been told their life depends on it.

The fear of uncertainty is the first example of a severely outdated program that our minds use to keep us safe. Being aware of this flawed programming is crucial to our experience as these fears come up, and we need a foundation from which to challenge them. The fear of uncertainty always questions our level of safety in any given moment. That is why safety is the consideration that directly impacts our ability to make good decisions.

Sometimes, when you are faced with the need to move forward, something unfamiliar surfaces in your life, bringing with it all this fear. If you do not understand its source, under these circumstances it's very hard to make an informed decision to move forward, because you are trying to do so in the face of everything inside you yelling that it is not safe, stay here, go back.

As human beings we always prefer to take on the demons we know rather than the ones we do not know. This is why we find comfort in familiarity. Even if we feel miserable, at least it is familiar and bearable. Why would I try something new and end up in a situation that might be more miserable than this? You might think you are playing a game of life based on creativity and exploration, but the program is running a game called fight for survival. This is one reason why so many books have been written on the topic of getting outside your comfort zone.

We believe it's much easier to deal with these types of fears when we understand their source. As a society, we spend far too much time demonizing fear instead of being grateful for the purpose fear serves, which is to keep us safe. The best way to deal with fear is from a place of gratitude and love. Long-term, it is impossible to overcome fear by putting a larger fear on top of it. Instead of paying so much attention to overcoming our fears, we need to give more attention to understanding the source of our fear.

2. Fear of Instant, Certain Death

There are no real surprises here. We fear things and actions that will kill us, so we avoid them. The advantage we have here is, as a species, we have spent eons mapping out and putting warning signs and fences around things that will kill us. Our ancestors were not so lucky; they had to figure it out for themselves.

3. Our Biggest Fear

Our biggest fear: You're going to die in a very short period of time, you don't know how, you don't know when, and it's most likely going to be excruciatingly painful. To explain this one, we go back again to the time in our species's evolution when we existed in packs and our only safety was in numbers. It took five people with sticks to fight off a bear or many other predators. You could not survive on your own. If you got kicked out of the pack, it meant you were going to die in a short period of time, likely from being eaten, which was going to be excruciatingly painful.

Our biggest fear is ugly death, but the experience that makes the fear real is rejection. Deep in our mind, rejection dooms us to a fate much worse than certain death. The first time we suffer a notable rejection, this fear kicks in and we feel vulnerable and alone. This sets off another program, and the fight for our survival has just begun. In ancient times when we were rejected from the pack we could only survive in one of two ways: either by regaining the acceptance of the pack in the hope they would let us back in, or through asserting domination and control by conquering the pack leader and becoming the new leader. If these two options sound familiar, it's because they resemble what we still do today. We are either seeking validation from others or to dominate and control them. Most of the major issues we deal with in the world today stem from those two dynamics.

Now you understand an underlying reason why it is so scary to be rejected. This is also why we are constantly trying to prove ourselves or control others. If you go back through your life, you will most likely see this fear as the underlying force behind almost everything you do. You were either moving toward validation or trying to exert control while, at the same time, trying to avoid rejection at all costs. Sometimes, to avoid the pain, you might even have turned to addiction and checked out of playing the game. This is when we adopt the belief that we are not good enough.

But this whole process is based on a lie. Rejection does not put our survival at risk—not even close. Almost nothing in modern times threatens our survival. You could be stripped of all your possessions and money and be kicked out of your house, and you would likely still survive. Your survival is rarely at stake, but your mind believes that it is. That is why we feel like life is a fight, because deep down we think we are always fighting for our survival.

If your survival is not really at risk, life does not have to be a fight. That means you are free to do anything you would like, depending on the quality of life you seek. We mistakenly believe it's rejection that puts our survival at risk, but in reality, the lie that sits underneath is fear itself. Being scared from time to time is perfectly normal, but if you are constantly living in fear, you are living a lie.

If our fears come from our evolution, where does our mind get all the other information we use to define our life and experiences? From our past, and a whole lot of that comes from our childhood.

PART
TWO

THE END OF
NEVERLAND

THE LOSS OF INNOCENCE AND WONDER

STORIES

Steph: *Childhood*

Growing up, I had a happy family and a pretty normal childhood. I constantly played outside. I had a lot of hobbies like riding my bike and playing on baseball teams. I also had a great imagination and loved to play that I was a grown-up. I loved school and had several friends. I had a great Barbie collection. All these things were so much fun growing up. Shortly after I turned eight, all of that changed.

While outside one day playing, my friends and I ran into an older boy in the neighborhood. I believe he was in high school. He called us over and somehow I got separated from my friends. He took me in his backyard, dragged me into his garage, pulled my pants down and molested me. When he was finished, he threatened me and told me it was my fault. He told me if I were to reveal what happened to anyone, he would say I made him do it.

I was so young I didn't know what sexual abuse was, but I knew I felt awful afterwards, and I knew it was wrong. I felt so ashamed and dirty.

After a few weeks of pure self-torture and worry, I decided I was going to tell my parents. One Saturday morning, I had just gotten up the courage to tell my dad. He was outside cleaning the garage and I was ready to tell him. Then the boy actually showed up to my house on his bike. I was freaking out; my heart was pounding, and I felt like I could have passed out. I was like, oh my God, he knows I'm going to tell. In reality, he had come to my house to see if my parents would buy some pizza for a fundraiser.

My dad went into the house to get his wallet to buy the pizza from him. The boy threatened me again saying, "Don't you ever tell. If you do, I will say you made me do it and your parents will believe me."

I was just eight years old and extremely terrified. I didn't know if my parents would believe me over him. I took this into my life and never told anyone until I was an adult. I grew up feeling lost, alone, and scared. I felt somehow this was my fault and I often blamed myself and wondered what I had done to have this happen to me. I didn't know how I could I go on living and be happy again when I had to carry this secret around.

Holding the secret caused deep worry and fear. I remember standing in front of the mirror thinking how dirty I felt and how much I hated myself and my body. This moment in front of the mirror ended up being a very defining part of my life. It was the moment I realized I didn't have a voice and, because of all the fear and mental distress I faced, I was never going to have one, either. When the boy threatened me, it stayed with me over and over again in my mind. It reinforced the fear and the fact that I was never going to tell. I felt like I didn't matter. I was a ghost nobody could truly see. I saw myself separate from my body, and it became this object I feared. I didn't know then that this happens to so many people. I thought I was odd and the only one. If I had only known I was not alone, that other people felt the same pain, maybe my life would have taken a different turn.

James: *Kindergarten*

My earliest memories from childhood are from about preschool age. From what I remember, I had a really happy childhood. I played a lot with my older brother. When my mom describes my childhood, she says I was one of those people who lit up the room when they walked in, someone who was full of life and got super excited about everything.

When my older brother went to school, I wanted to go so bad I would beg my mom every day to let me go with him. On my first day of school, I can remember the excitement I felt, but after I got there it became apparent I had some pretty severe learning disabilities. I struggled with reading. I was tested and put in a special education class.

The first day I was to go to special education class, my teacher called me up in front of the room and said, "Jimmy, I don't know if you know this or not, but only stupid and retarded kids go to special ed." I was shocked. I didn't know what to think. I just kind of froze. When I turned to walk out of class, she told the entire class to tell me I was stupid on the way out.

I told my mom all about it when I got home that night, but she was undiagnosed manic depressive, with a mental illness that is now called bipolar disorder. She wasn't really capable of taking on a situation of that magnitude. She told me the world is a cruel place and there are a lot of mean people out there. She told me I just had to learn to deal with it and do the best I could.

The next day I went to school hoping what had happened was just a one-time occurrence. But every single day for the rest of my kindergarten year, my teacher would call me up in front of the class, tell me I was stupid, then make the entire class call me stupid. I instinctively knew I couldn't show any emotions to those people and, if I did, it would mean trouble for me. It was at that point that I detached from my emotions.

My teacher had given the kids permission to bully me. One kid named Scott, the teacher's pet, took the lead. For the next couple of years, he became my personal bully. He would follow me everywhere just to make fun of me. I knew I couldn't let him, or the other kids, see me cry.

My parents got divorced when I was three years old and my dad's involvement in my life became very sporadic. He wasn't around to help me because he was off partying. He spent most of his time smoking weed and hanging out with friends. He failed to pay my mom child support, so we grew up poor. All my clothes were hand-me-downs from my brother, which didn't help with my bullying situation at school.

My dad was supposed to pick me up every other week to spend the weekend with him. Every Friday I would call him and ask, "Dad, are you coming to get me?" "I'm coming right now." "You Promise? "Yes, I'll be there in 30 minutes." I would get so excited I would go out and wait on the porch for him until I fell asleep. My mom would come and get me and drag me back into the house. She would always make up some kind of excuse, like "Your dad called and said couldn't make it tonight, but he'll be here first thing in the morning."

That was hard for me. I felt rejected. This guy should have loved me and wanted to spend time with me, but he didn't. Why would he lie to me like that? This wasn't something that happened once; it seemed like it happened a thousand times. It was confusing because as a kid I would ask myself, *What is wrong with me? Why doesn't he want to spend time with me?* Every time he did it, I wanted to believe him so bad, I would run out to the porch every weekend and sit there, waiting. My dad would either show up late at night, or he wouldn't come at all.

Steph: *The New Normal*

Shortly after my abuse, I noticed that my house seemed very chaotic. My parents weren't getting along. I was the middle child, but I always seemed to be the one in the room or the car when they were fighting. To this day, I cannot emotionally handle people arguing and shouting. I grew up believing relationships were dysfunctional and hard.

All the chaos in my parents' relationship is probably the reason why they didn't notice there was something wrong with me. They couldn't see my sadness, because they had their own set of issues to deal with. They ended up getting a divorce when I was nine years old, and somehow, over and over, I always thought it was my fault. I couldn't stop blaming myself for my parents' issues.

The divorce and my mom's remarriage uprooted my life, and it completely changed, in a way that I could never have imagined. We moved away and I lost everything I knew: my friends, my school, and the home I grew up in. We ended up moving to a little town in the country, the kind of town that only has two stoplights. I don't know if you have ever been to a small town, and no offense if you live in one. But I am a true city girl, and this was a total culture shock to me! Everyone knows everyone and their business, and that can make you feel like even more of an outsider. I felt alienated. I did have some friends, but I struggled to fit in, and I never felt comfortable showing anyone the real me. I always wanted to portray someone different, because I thought the real me wasn't good enough.

My dad and I used to be very close. After my parents got divorced, I only saw my dad a handful of times. The times I did see him were extremely chaotic. One time my brother and I went to stay at his house. We were watching TV and my dad asked us if we wanted to go to dinner. We all got into the car, and on the way there he said he had to stop by and say hello to a friend. He pulled into the parking lot of a strip bar and left us alone in the car for a couple of hours. I remember being so angry that he just left us in the car starving and waiting for him, which seemed like an eternity. After he returned it was midnight and he took us to eat with some random lady at a Denny's. Looking back, it's clear to me that the only reason he asked us to dinner was so he could go to the bar. Whenever it seemed like he had good intentions, the part of him that didn't give a shit about us just took over. I remember another time when he came to see us and he brought a girlfriend. He kept bragging about her, and he boasted over the fact that she was a stripper. He even gave us wallet-size photos of her posing almost naked. My mother was appalled and threw the photos out, but every so often he would give us more photos of her. I don't know if he was proud that he was dating a stripper, or if he was just trying to get back at my mom because she divorced him. Another time I went to his house and he left me alone for a really long time and didn't come back. The next day I called my mom and she told me to get into a cab and go to my grandparents' house because it was only twenty minutes away. I didn't understand why before the divorce he had seemed to be such a caring and loving parent, and now he was gone. After that, he called a few times, but we would just end up getting into arguments because he never showed up when he said he was going to, and eventually he didn't even pretend to care. He always had an excuse as to why he wouldn't come to get us.

He did not contact me again until I was an adult. He made a very fake attempt at having a relationship with me. I saw him a couple of times over the course of a few months. He invited me over to his house to meet his girlfriend, who was, ironically enough, only one year older than me. She had three little kids, and he actually had the nerve to say to me, "I help raise her kids because their dad is a piece of shit and never sees them." Right then and there it felt as if someone had just punched me right in the face, and it reaffirmed all the pain that I felt my entire life. I only saw him one more time after that, and he told me that he had left that woman and her kids. And then he just disappeared out of my life, again, off the face of the earth.

If the one person in the world who was supposed to love me didn't, to me this meant I was unlovable. It was really heartbreaking to grow up knowing that my own dad didn't love me. I felt like he was just out living his life, while my world was growing darker, and he had no clue how much pain I was in. It took me several years to heal from all the feelings of rejection and pain that he caused me.

I am now at a point in my life when I have healed and realize that he didn't leave because of me, he left because of the sadness that he felt inside himself. It's sad how many years I agonized over the belief that he left because of me. Now he is missing out on my life, and he has no idea how many amazing grandchildren he has, and that's his loss.

James: *Never Again*

At the end of my kindergarten year, I convinced my mom to call the school and take me out of my special education class. I was never going to be humiliated that way again for being different or stupid. I never went back to special ed. But as I moved forward with my life, being pulled out of special ed presented its own problems. I needed help because I had severe dyslexia. Reading was difficult and spelling was impossible for me.

I literally slipped through the cracks all the way through school. I know in today's world this story is almost unbelievable. But at that time, they didn't test kids at each grade level as rigorously as they do today.

Just think, if it is difficult for an adult to wrap their mind around this, imagine how hard it must have been for me as a child. Here was a person in a position of authority telling me every single day that I was stupid and not good enough. What choice did I have but to believe her? This was a very emotional experience for me. Even though I didn't show the emotions, I certainly felt them. Over time, I just became numb to it. I came to believe that I was stupid, because the teacher had told me so.

Moving forward from that experience, I never felt like I was going to be good enough. I felt rejected by everyone. It really established a low image for me. I don't remember a lot from my childhood. I couldn't name five teachers that I had. But I certainly remember that one, her name, and exactly what she looked like. I remember the boy who bullied me, his name, and what he looked like. Those memories are burned deeply into my subconscious mind.

One day, I was in the school bathroom, standing at the urinal, and that boy who was bullying me saw my underwear. My grandmother had bought me underwear with racing cars pictured on them. He looked at my underwear and screamed, "Jimmy's got flowers on his underwear. Jimmy wears girls' underwear." It was the first time that I ever really tried to defend myself. He was screaming this outside and I ran out shouting, "They are racing cars." But he didn't care if they were flowers or racing cars. He kept saying to all the other kids that I wore girls' underwear. He just used this as another opportunity to make fun of me. I stopped defending myself at that point. As the kids stood in a circle, chanting how "Jimmy wears girls' underwear," my best friend at the time, whose name I don't even remember, whispered in my ear, "If I don't make fun of you, they will make fun of me." And I said, Okay, I get it, just do what you have to do.

On the elementary school playground one day, during second grade, I climbed up one of those old tall slides. All around it was hard-packed dirt. I was standing on the top, yelling to somebody, and the next thing I remember I woke up in the hospital. There was so much damage to the left side of my face that my mom said I looked like the elephant boy. I was out of school for a week or two because my face was swollen up and I couldn't even see, especially out of my left eye. I didn't know how it happened, because I was knocked unconscious when I hit the ground. I found out later, from a friend, that I was pushed off that slide. I made a choice not to tell my mom what had really happened.

As a result of these experiences, I knew that I wasn't safe. I felt alone. Nobody had my back. Nobody was there for me. In a sense, nobody cared.

I had to find a way to survive. Survival was the only thing that mattered. I was unlovable. I was a reject. If I was going to survive, I had to figure out a way to protect myself.

Years later, it became clear that on the playground I was the most dominating athlete in the school. I went from being picked last in sports to being picked first, to being the team captain. If you wanted to win at dodgeball or anything else, you needed me on your team. Sports became my saving grace, and my sport of choice became baseball. My life revolved around it. My treatment by others improved over the next six years as I joined baseball teams. That gave me more acceptance from the other kids and helped me to break free of the bullying.

But something changed when I got into high school and started playing baseball. I couldn't hit the ball anymore, and I started missing pop flies in the outfield. I began to think I wasn't as good as I once thought I was, which was a real blow, because I had tied my entire identity to being in sports. I was still struggling in school and I had my self-esteem tied to the one thing I thought I was good at, which was baseball. I was convinced I would be a professional baseball player someday, but all of a sudden, I couldn't play well anymore. The only place where I felt acceptance was now ripped away. When you're the best, everyone loves you; when you can't play, nobody cares about you. I was pushed back into isolation.

Many years later I found out, while taking a driver's test, that I couldn't see well out of my left eye, which had been injured in my fall from the slide. I was almost legally blind in my left eye from a cataract that had developed, which explained my poor performance in baseball.

When you think about it, the bullies did win, because they took away baseball, the one thing I was good at. I didn't have any other real skills to depend on or push me forward in life. From that point forward, the bullying started up again, and my self-esteem crashed.

CHAPTER

5

IDENTITY CRISIS

FEAR OF REJECTION

At some point in life, everyone suffers from what they view as a major rejection. The world shouts "you are not good enough" in your face, and brands your spirit with the imprint of trauma and separation. It is at this point that you have an identity crisis and your life spins in a totally different direction. It's called survival mode.

In these moments you begin to perceive and believe that life is not the playground you once believed it to be, and that you will need to fight to survive. It is also when you realize that you are separate and alone.

The rejection and belief that we are not good enough splits in our mind, showing up in four different ways. The ego takes over and starts the drive for acceptance and control. Why? Even though we live in a world where our survival is no longer at stake from moment to moment, our minds are running an outdated survival program. Remember our earlier discussion, about how back in the day when we lived in tribes, rejection from the tribe meant certain and ugly death.

This knowledge is encoded deep inside us. At that level of consciousness, rejection literally means an ugly death, which is why we have such a hard time with it. When we experience harsh rejection for the first time, it kicks off this primal programming, which tells us that if we do not gain acceptance or control immediately, we will die.

Such an identity crisis will cause you to question everyone and everything, most of all yourself. To add to the confusion, your authentic self goes into hiding. Your life is no longer your own because you are now trying to live up to what you think everyone else wants you to be. This causes chaos inside you as you start to obsess about what other people think of you. You quickly lose your sense of wonder and awe. Imagination falls by the wayside as you begin to think it's a game that only kids can afford to play. And for the first time in your life, you contemplate what it means to be alone.

From this point forward, your life becomes a fight for survival. This fight shows up in the following four ways

IS THIS GOOD ENOUGH? AND SO ON

When your bubble of childhood innocence bursts, an internal shift happens, and the first thing you decide is that you need to become someone different from your authentic self. Because of that belief, you start to morph and change to cover up your true nature, in an attempt to become what you think the world wants you to be. At this point your ego takes over, spins up a new persona, presents that persona as the new and improved you, offers it to the world, seeks validation, and hopes to gain acceptance.

Once you start shifting to become something different, you keep shifting. You shift as many times as necessary in order to gain the acceptance you believe you need deep down in order to survive. When you cannot gain the acceptance you desire, you either keep trying endlessly or you choose another path, which is to attempt to control those who you believe are rejecting you. Or you can check out of the process through addiction or suicide.

Because you are made to feel that the authentic version of yourself isn't inherently good enough, that part goes into hiding. The problem is that you will never gain the acceptance that you desire: Because you are trying to gain acceptance for a persona, not for your authentic self, it causes a massive conflict inside of you; you can never feel whole until you embrace the truth about yourself, but the truth is now buried under multiple personas. As long as you are ignoring what and who you really are, you will never gain acceptance from the person you need it from the most to end this cycle, and of course that is you.

Ask yourself this question: What if I am everything that I think that I'm not . . . and nothing that I think that I am?

The truth in that question can be found by identifying the areas of your life where you suffered major rejection, and as a result, feel like you are not good enough. Those parts of your life always feel like a struggle. When you choose to believe that you are not good enough, you lose access to your authentic self. Basically, you are living a lie, and no matter how real you make that lie seem, it is still a lie.

In the areas of your life where you are struggling, there is a lie sitting at the core of who you are. And that is why it doesn't matter how much money you have, and it doesn't matter how much success you achieve. If you don't go back and question the lie, you will never be truly happy.

THE SPLIT: SEPARATION

The second thing this rejection does is cause you to adopt the belief of separation, creating a *me vs. you* scenario. Back in the early days of our existence there was no concept of I. Most primitive cultures did not even have a word for I; there was only we. It's just like when you're a young child and you don't see yourself as separate from your parents. Because of rejection, for the first time in your life you see yourself as separate. This is when you start perceiving everything through the eyes of fear. You are now on high alert all the time. The idea of separation causes you to feel lonely in a room full of people.

The lie of separation, in some ways, is the most damaging one. Though our survival as a species means we are completely dependent on one another, the idea of separation is at the heart of every war, every argument, and every disagreement. It is the main cause of loneliness, depression, and other mental illness. When you see yourself as separate it causes you to falsely believe in the idea of scarcity, that there is never enough of anything—ever. In order for someone to win, someone else has to lose. This is the idea that supports putting a price on a life.

When scarcity becomes the norm, people never look at the long-term consequences of their actions. They do not care about anything but themselves. Which makes perfect sense when put into the right light. When a survival mechanism is triggered inside you, survival becomes the only thing that matters. When you are living in a place of survival, you lead a "hand-to-mouth" existence. You are not thinking about the survival of the species, or the planet, or even about your own grandchildren, for that matter. You are alone fighting for your life and the life of your family. Period. Nothing else matters.

Just to be clear, if it were true that your survival was on the line, all these behaviors would be perfectly normal and acceptable. But because you believe it is true, it is true for you. That is why it is so important to understand what is going on, and to question the lie underneath.

YOU NOW HAVE A SHADOW

The third thing that happens is the creation of your shadow self. When you are rejected, you feel others' contempt for the first time. You adopt a victim mentality because what just happened seems very much out of your control. Left unchecked, your shadow will be the cancer that destroys your life.

Once the cycle of blame starts, it is very hard to end. If you are a person who internalizes, this is where the punishment starts. You begin endlessly beating yourself up to the point where you start hating yourself. You blame yourself for everything bad that has ever happened to you. You feel unlovable, all the while you just want someone to love and accept you. But it has never happened because you do not accept yourself. This darkness builds inside of you until you feel like you can't take the pain anymore. You might even reach the point of taking your pain out on yourself or others.

If you are somebody who externalizes your emotions, you start pointing the finger at the world and blaming everyone and everything else for why your life is not working out. At first, you seek sympathy, just looking for people to understand your pain and frustration and to confirm that the world is a cruel place and what they did to you was unjust. If you can't find people to sympathize with you, your frustration builds, and you start lashing out, looking for love and attention, but what you get most often is more rejection. In extreme cases the people in this situation often end up addicted or incarcerated.

If you are one of the lucky ones, you learn to live with the shadow, you learn to manage it. Some people even figure out a way to find strength in the darkness. But it's always there lurking, waiting for its chance to pop its ugly head out. It always seems to pop out at the worst possible times and places. When it does, you feel embarrassed and ashamed, and you once again tuck it away. It still lives inside you, patiently waiting to emerge another day.

TOP IT ALL OFF WITH SHAME

A fourth thing that happens when you get rejected is the introduction of shame. You feel shame about who you are, but you feel even more shame about the person you feel like you are now being forced to become. Because the failure and rejection is causing you to run full speed away from the authentic version of you, you are also ashamed of abandoning your true authentic self.

Our awareness of ourselves and the world starts to close down, and our reactions become defensive. The shame we feel starts to shift how we feel about ourselves and the world around us. Let's use children as an example. When they are young, they are full of light and love; after they suffer rejection or a series of rejections, their light dims or goes out altogether. Most of us just write this process off as a child's exposure to the harsh realities of life. But rejection inflicts a deeper trauma and makes them feel shame for who they are.

The shame we feel is what makes the light of possibility fade from our eyes. We are shocked when we find out that we are not good enough, or that people don't like us. We accept these things as truths, and we start living the consequences of believing the lies.

PART THREE

WELCOME
TO THE MATRIX

IT WAS OVER BEFORE IT STARTED

STORIES

James: The Smell of Desperation

As I moved into the dating age, I just wanted somebody to make me feel better, somebody to love me. I needed to feel accepted because I was super desperate for love. I didn't realize it at the time, but desperation is not a turn-on for girls. I might as well have been wearing a T-shirt that said PLEASE DON'T DATE ME. I WAS repelling girls.

Whenever I did manage to get a girlfriend, the relationship wouldn't last very long. I couldn't understand it. I also picked the absolute worst friends. I was so desperate I would engage with anybody who would talk with me. It was a constant theme in my life that the people I chose to be my friends would screw me over in some way. They would talk shit behind my back and backstab me at work or with a girl. I put my trust in the wrong people and it always cost me. This became a trend in my life and reinforced my underlying belief that the world is a shitty place and people are bad. I wanted to believe people are good, but my underlying beliefs and perception continued to show me people are bad.

When I did date girls, I dated girls who would cheat on me with the guys I was hanging out with. It was one heartbreak after another, yet I kept trusting people. One of the reasons I did this and felt so confused was because my mom went to church a lot, and I kept hearing over and over again, be a good person, be nice, be kind, and good things will happen to you. This wasn't my experience. I tried to be friendly and nice, but every time I put trust in someone, it blew up in my face.

As I started getting jobs, they proved difficult for me because I had to avoid skill sets I hadn't learned in school. I got through school by talking a good game and convincing my teachers I was a great person. I spent a lot of time developing relationships so they would know that even if I wasn't doing the work correctly, I was smart enough to pass the class. In the end, they would feel sorry for me, and like me enough not to fail me. This always worked, with the exception of one class in high school.

I thought that same likability would carry through into the workplace, but it just didn't. For one thing, I was an atrocious speller, and I had to be careful not do anything to give anyone a reason to think I was stupid. I had to find jobs in construction, painting, or working as a waiter in restaurants. Jobs I didn't care about and didn't want to be doing the rest of my life.

Most people have something in their life that works. I didn't seem to have anything. I didn't have any decent relationships. I tried to keep my chin up, but I started to give up hope. I grew very frustrated and bitter. Anger started to own me.

I saw happy people around me, people who had great lives, but I couldn't comprehend why my own life was such a struggle. I just couldn't connect the dots. Nothing made sense to me. Was God punishing me? Was I going to be the butt of the joke or a victim forever? I didn't know. I just knew I was losing my trust in humanity. I began to feel like the bullies had won and I had lost. I felt they had stomped my light out and I was never going to have the life I desired. I had been beaten into sub-mission by life.

I was in pain. In order to cope with the pain, I began doing drugs. At first, it was casual, a little cocaine on the weekend. I thought I had con-trol of it. I felt better because it made me feel numb. I turned to crystal meth for a while as a way to feel better and get the energy to get through the days. As time went on, using once or twice a week became once or twice a day. I was an addict. Cocaine became crack, snorting crystal meth became shooting crystal meth, and, eventually, heroin. I wasn't a very picky addict. I took whatever was available, anything to help me escape the pain I was feeling.

Everything started deteriorating around me. I got to the point where drugs became my whole life; not just my escape, but my very existence. Soon I was passing bad checks all over town and bad experiences started stacking up. I just didn't give a shit about anything anymore.

One drug dealer I stole from trapped me in a house. I escaped and he chased me for miles. I found out later that this same drug dealer killed someone else in a similar situation. Had he caught me, I would have been dead. That's the kind of life I was leading.

Steph: *Angry and Alone*

I think my mother always wondered why I was such a sad soul, or maybe just wondered what was wrong with me. As I moved into my teenage years, my mom and I were constantly at each other's throats. I didn't know how to talk to her, so arguing was just easier. I was so angry because she was trying to move on with her life. I felt stuck and alone, like I was being left behind, and I hated her for it. Eventually I refused to communicate with her, and she didn't seem to mind.

Not speaking up about my abuse caused me to completely withdraw from life. Looking back at photos of me, there is a sadness in my face. I refused to smile in any picture because I felt so empty inside. I thought I would be acting fake if I smiled for the camera. I struggled to find my place in the world, and I really started to adopt the belief that I didn't belong here.

I became more and more angry. As time went on, I started lashing out. I wasn't getting the attention I needed. I felt angry and, because of this, I started to cut myself. One day my mom and I got into a fight and I went into the house and took a razor blade and cut my leg open. The wound was so bad I had to get stitches. I felt drawn to hurting myself because I just wanted to feel something and hoped that maybe it would get me some attention. I was in so much pain inside. I didn't care if I physically hurt myself because it hurt less than the emotional pain I lived with constantly.

I was never taught how to share my feelings or what my emotions meant. I didn't have the tools or the knowledge that my feelings and emotions were an indicator something was wrong. Because of my abuse, I was terrified of speaking up. I taught myself to shove my emotions and feelings deep down inside, because when they came up, I could not physically handle the pain they caused.

My body image was distorted. Even though I was a size 0, all I could see was the fat on my body. I became obsessed. One day I was watching TV and I saw an after-school special on eating disorders. These specials were intended to inform kids and help them not make the same mistakes, but I had the opposite reaction and thought it was a great idea. I could eat whatever I wanted and just throw it up. I wouldn't have to worry about what I ate and could still stay skinny. As I became bulimic, it was all I could think about. It consumed my life. If we went out to eat as a family, all I could think about was whether or not there was going to be a bathroom where I could throw up. I knew I would be suffering if I had to hold it down the whole car ride home.

I was a wild teenager; I did whatever I wanted. The rare times I came home by curfew, I would say goodnight, run to my room and sneak right out of my bedroom window. I often got into trouble, but I never cared. I felt entitled to do whatever I wanted, and I didn't care about being punished. I figured if my family didn't give a shit about me, I wasn't going to care about them or their rules. This was back in the day when there weren't any cell phones, so my mom couldn't find me. I just lied about where I was and what I had been doing and there was no evidence. I was always out with boys and friends, but mostly boys because I just wanted someone to love me. I thought if I gave them what they wanted, they would love me. It didn't work out that way. Because I felt damaged, I always picked the wrong guys and attracted guys who were totally broken.

I moved out the second I could, hoping for a better life. Instead, things got worse. I dated terrible men who were abusers, jerks, drug users, alcoholics, and cheaters. I always thought I could fix them, which is funny considering I couldn't manage to fix myself. I felt no one loved me, but, more importantly, I didn't love myself. I kept wondering, what is wrong with me? Do I really deserve to have men treat me like shit? Why can't I find someone to love me?

I often looked up at the stars in the sky and wished someday I would be happy. As time went on, my world grew extremely dark and sad. I became extremely depressed and started to lose all hope about my future or of ever having any happiness in my life.

James: *Descending into Hell*

As my addiction grew, I lost my possessions and place to live. My entire life was falling apart. I had a friend who started off as casual party buddy, but eventually became my best friend. We used drugs together and both fell into addiction. After he was arrested for shoplifting, he went into drug treatment and was able to get sober for a while. Then one weekend, when his probation officer was out of town, he decided he wanted to party one last time. He called me on the phone and he sounded tired. I asked what he was doing. He said, "Nothing man, I miss you, want to see you. Come over and hang out with me." I told him I'd come as soon as I could.

It took me a while to get over to his house. I knocked on his door and could see him through the window slumped over on the bed. I kicked in the door, but as I got closer I could see he was purple and already gone. There are a lot of things drugs take away from you, but there is nothing more painful than losing the people you love the most. I felt extremely guilty for not going straight over there and I beat myself up for not recognizing the signs when I was on the phone with him. I just thought he sounded tired. I was heartbroken and stopped caring about anyone or anything.

Eventually, I lost everything. I did anything necessary to support my addiction. I started buying enough drugs to sell to offset the cost of my own addiction, but as my addiction grew, it became more expensive and I started committing small crimes like shoplifting and passing bad checks.

I destroyed every relationship I had. I didn't care; I was checked out. The only time I felt bad and felt in pain was when I was sober. I did whatever it took to get the drugs I needed so I didn't have to feel the pain.

Over time I created some serious enemies. I even had a hit put out on me by a guy who thought I had stolen from him when, ironically, I hadn't. He hired two gang members fresh out of prison to kill me. To this day, I don't know how I survived. I didn't know what was coming when they pulled up behind my car, drew their guns, and proceeded to dump 15 rounds apiece into the back of my open Bronco. Then they chased me for blocks, and when they caught up to me, they did it again. I don't know how all those bullets missed me, but I managed to get away.

As my crimes accumulated, the police came after me. I got arrested several times but always got out on bail. Then I got thrown in jail again, only this time it was apparent I wasn't going to get out. A police officer came and offered to release me if I helped him find someone who ran in my same drug circles. I agreed and he put an ankle tracker on me. Once I was out, I cut off the tracker and went on the run.

I avoided capture for three months, but when they finally caught me, they were pissed. I was put in their super max unit, solitary confinement. I was locked in a box all alone and only allowed out for one hour every other day. I was trapped and had no idea how long I was going to be there.

Steph: *The Darkness Consumed Me*

How do we get to the point where we want to take our own lives?

When I got to that hotel room, I wanted to die more than anything. It consumed all of me. I had spent years internalizing the pain, and my perception of life was so distorted that I literally couldn't see or feel any love. In my mind, I was unlovable, unwanted, and didn't belong on this planet. When I took out that piece of paper, I couldn't think of a single reason to stay and could only see a million reasons to go. Living with the fact of being abandoned repeatedly made me feel like my life didn't have any value. I wasn't able to see them any other way because I couldn't see past my pain and the fact that I was physically abandoned by my dad and felt emotionally abandoned by my mom. My mom did the best she could, but she was trying to move on with her life. She was remarried and was trying to put all her efforts into her marriage. She couldn't see how much pain I was in and I couldn't see that she just wanted to be happy. We had a lot of resentment toward each other because I felt abandoned by her and she probably felt like I was an asshole teenager—and I was. I didn't know that my dark perception of myself had clouded my ability to see the differences between healthy and unhealthy relationships. I didn't know people could actually be truly happy together or get along. I didn't have anyone I could turn to. I tried to find love, but I hated myself and attracted men who hated themselves. Like attracts like, and I ended up with people who felt just as sad, lonely, and depressed as I was. Those relationships were all awful because things don't generally get better when two broken people get together. That day in the hotel I had left a relationship because it was abusive. We were constantly fighting and neither one of us had the knowledge or understanding of how to change ourselves. I thought all relationships were messy and chaotic because my parents' broken relationship was still fresh in my mind. If this was all my life was ever going to be, I didn't want to be here to experience any more pain. It hurt so much to be alive. I didn't want to face my life anymore, and I definitely couldn't stare at my own inadequacies for a second longer.

SEEING IS NOT BELIEVING

PERCEPTION AND EMOTION

Have you ever wondered how life works? I think we all ask ourselves this from time to time. The answer to this question is not a mystery. It has been right in front of us for a long time, but very few people are talking about it. We seem to be fumbling around in the dark because we believe we don't have any insights into the function of life. The strange part is we seem to be obsessed with instruction books for everything else.

Here is why it matters to us collectively: We waste so much time figuring out the mechanics of how life works that we spend little time actually living it. One time, James bought a huge barbecue grill at the local home store. It was not put together, and James is not what you would consider a handyman. The instructions were terrible, and it took him five hours to put the monstrosity together. Reflecting back on the project, he realized he could put another one together in twenty minutes now that he understood how to do it. This is how it works for a lot of things in life.

There are two things that dictate your life experience. Everyone can describe what they are, yet most people don't fully understand how they work. These two things are perception and emotions.

As we said earlier, perception and emotions dictate all your experiences from beginning to end. Everything you are, everything you see, everything you experience, is dictated by perception. And your emotions are what give your life the only meaning it has. Together, perception and emotions form all our experiences, yet most of us don't seem to understand them. It's time to change that! Let's explore what they mean.

PERCEPTION: BELIEVING IS SEEING

If we asked you to describe what perception is, you would probably give the standard answer that perception is how we view the world. That would be right, but if we asked you how perception works, you probably wouldn't know. Most people don't, and that's the part we find confusing. Why? you ask. Because it clearly demonstrates that most people don't fully understand the role perception plays in life. If you did, not only would you want to understand, you would want to become an expert in it.

You might be thinking, Okay, what is this role that perception plays in my life that's so important? Perception literally is your life. Understanding how it works is the difference between driving in the dark and using your headlights.

How important is it, really? A few chapters ago we talked about the fact that you have never made a bad decision, you have only ever made decisions on the basis of bad information. Well, it's your perception that gives you all that bad information. What you may fail to realize is that the information you're using to decide the direction of your life is based on assumptions, and you know what they say about the word assume . . . it makes an ASS out of U and ME.

When someone says they try not to make assumptions, it sounds great, but that's not actually possible because of the way perception works. Life, and all the meaning you place on it, is based on assumptions. That is the way your mind evolved to interpret your experiences.

If this doesn't seem to make much sense, what we're going to say next is going to make even less. Here is the fundamental principle that underlies perception. You do not see reality. As a matter of fact, your experiences have no meaning except for the meaning you give them. As our neuroscientist friend, Beau Lotto, says: "There is a reality, but you just don't have access to it."

I'm sure some of you are scratching your head right now. We were too when we first tried to wrap our heads around this idea. A good place to start is to ask the question, "If we don't see reality, what do we see?"

What you see is an assumption. Your mind collects all the available information and makes a decision about what that information means. You only ever see your interpretation of what you think reality is, because that's all you have access to. You see an assumption because that's the way your mind works.

The next question you should probably ask is, "How close is my assumption to actual reality?" This varies widely from situation to situation and is based on the information you're using to make your assumption. If the information is good, then the assumption is good. If the information is off, then the assumption is off. If the assumption is off, then your decision will also be off.

The next question you should be asking is, "Where does my mind get the information to make these assumptions?" It gets it from the only place it can, your past. How does your mind decide which of your past experiences to use in any given situation to fuel your assumptions? That's the problem: There's no way of knowing. Memories with strong emotions tied to them seem to come up more often because the unprocessed emotion keeps them at the forefront of your mind. The fact that memories with strong emotional ties are used more often presents us with a whole new set of problems.

Here is an example: Imagine you have a six-year-old child, and every time you have a big decision to make, you hand it over to this child and allow them to make whatever decision they think is best. How do you think your life would turn out? If you don't take the time to understand perception, that is exactly what can happen. Because your perception sources your past to give meaning to the present, you have no idea how far back your mind has to go in any given situation to find the meaning it needs. This means you have zero conscious input about which version of you is going to have a say in your current situation. This is why fear plays such a huge role in our lives.

Let's use self-esteem as an example of how this works. Question: Would you like to have better self-esteem? I don't think anybody would ever say no to this. But why would you like to have better self-esteem? Most people would say it would make them more confident, they would show up differently in their life, and it would generally make everything better. Wouldn't you agree?

When you break down self-esteem, it is essentially your view of yourself. If this is true, if it is just your opinion, then you should be able to change it. But it's not that easy, because you don't know what the underlying beliefs are that make up your self-esteem, let alone how to change them.

Let's break it down. Most experts agree your self-esteem is established by the age of six. If your self-esteem has such a big impact on your daily experiences, that means your six-year-old self gets to decide, to a certain degree, how your life is going to turn out. This is the source of just one of many beliefs that are still tied to your childhood.

This is a fundamental problem we face. We don't understand what information goes into dictating our life's path. Now are you getting a sense of why it's so critical to understand perception?

Here is one of the most important things we have discovered. The next step to getting anything you want in life is already available to you. The possibilities are infinite. You just can't see them because you don't believe it is possible, because that's how *perception* works.

Question: What if the things you wanted most in life were sitting right in front of you and you just couldn't see them? Do you think that's possible? Not only is it possible, it happens all the time.

Think of a man who wants more than anything to find love. He wants to be in a relationship, but unfortunately, he has really low self-esteem. One day this man walks into a store. When he walks up to the counter, the girl working there starts to flirt. Does he recognize that the girl is flirting with him?

If you answered, as most people do, that no, he doesn't see it, then you already have a fundamental understanding of how perception works.

This guy was just given the opportunity to get the thing he wants most in the world and he missed it, even though it was right in front of him. The question you should be asking yourself is, what if that's happening to me? What if you are missing the opportunity to get the things you want most in the world?

It's happening to you every single day. It happens to us all, because that is the way perception works.

Why do you think the man didn't see the opportunity? Like we said, it's because he has low self-esteem. Why does that matter? Why would his low self-esteem have any impact on the reality going on outside him? For the same reason you can't see the things you want. He does not believe it's possible.

Why can't we see things we do not believe are possible? It's actually pretty simple. When we don't think something is possible, our perception isn't looking for it, and therefore we don't see it. As our minds process volumes of information, our perception does not give priority to things we do not think are possible. It's the same reason why we wouldn't go looking for a pot of gold at the end of a rainbow.

Our biggest issue is we fail to realize that the opportunity to get everything we want is already there. It's just sitting outside our awareness. We can't see it because we don't believe it. We live in a world of infinite possibilities. In every minute of life, anything is possible if we believe it. We believe our life is dictated by the things we see, but, actually, it's dictated more by the things we don't see.

The law of attraction, vision boards, and the power of positive thinking work because they help you to believe what you want is possible. They help you see more of the opportunities that are already available. The power of intention will move you subconsciously toward the things you want and the people who can help you get them, but you will never see those things until you believe that. This is the secret sauce.

Perception, like eyesight, has a limited field. We call this your field of perception. Your field of perception works on a scale; the more you believe it, the better the chance you have to see it. The further down the scale, the less likely you are to see it. This is why you can only see what you believe is possible.

Your perception dictates what information you can see by setting up priorities for the information that's coming in. These priorities can shift from second to second. They are based on many things, from belief to the mood you're in. If you're in a positive state, you will see something different than if you're in a negative state. A fear-based state throws the whole system into flux and you see something totally different.

Let's consider the impact of positive thinking on perception. There is a lot of scientific backing to the impact of thought on perception, some of which you will find in the reference material at the end of this book. What always comes up when you talk about positive thinking are the pessimists who say things like, "I'm not a pessimist, I'm a realist. I like to deal in facts. I don't want to dilute myself with all this positive thinking mumbo-jumbo."

Unfortunately, the pessimist fails to realize how perception works. They, like everybody else, have no access to reality. Their pessimistic view is just a construct of their mind and is no more based in reality than a positive view. The difference is, a pessimistic view severely limits their field of perception and the number of opportunities they can see.

Positive thinking opens up our field of perception because, when we are in a positive state of mind, we are open to new possibilities. This is why when we adopted the belief that everything happens in our best interest, we began to see a positive shift in our lives.

When something bad or difficult happened in our lives, we would just tell ourselves that everything happens in our best interest. This kept our field of perception open instead of jumping into the negativity of the circumstances surrounding us. This allowed us to see opportunities in negative events. In other words, when negative events happened, we were always looking for the positive that was going to come out of it and always found new opportunities available to us.

You can continue viewing the world from a negative viewpoint, but it will cost you. Whenever you choose a negative view, your field of perception starts to close and you start to lose the ability to see the infinite possibilities that surround you every day. When you choose a more positive mindset, which we admit takes a lot of hard work, you open your field of perception and start to see opportunities you never dreamed were possible. The long and short of it is, negativity closes down, while positivity opens up.

Let's keep exploring other ways in which perception works. Your mind is a vast database of memories that are categorized into beliefs. Beliefs are decisions you make about your world through the process of mapping your environment. Beliefs are what fuel your perception.

When you have an experience, your mind does something similar to a Google search. Your mind races through your memories to find the most similar experience to the one you are experiencing now. It then applies the same meaning to the current experience as it did to the similar experience. You are not seeing reality because your past is always being projected onto your present.

When you heard the story about the man's perception in the store, you knew it was true, but you don't think the same thing is happening to you. At least not very often. This is where you are wrong, it happens to you all the time. It happens to all of us and is core to the human experience.

Your brain can process millions of bits of information a second, far more than your conscious mind can handle. Your mind, through your perception, takes all that information and compresses it down to just a few bits of information that are then delivered to your conscious mind. The problem is how your mind decides what the most important pieces of information are for you to focus on.

Your mind's core programming, or belief system, develops from a combination of evolution and environment. These ideas are an extremely mixed bag, with tons of contradictions. You have a certain set of beliefs in one area of your life and a completely contradictory set in another area.

If you want to change for the better, stop asking yourself what you need to do differently and start asking yourself what you need to perceive differently. This is a skill that must be fostered and trained because, in life, interpretation is everything.

We also need to consider how evolution affects your perception.

Here is where it gets tricky. It's not just your past that generates priorities, it's also human evolution. What is perception's main priority from an evolutionary standpoint? It is survival! Your perception does not care if you are happy, successful, creative, or fulfilled. It does not care what your dreams are or whether or not you have a great life. It evolved to do one job and one job only. It evolved to keep you safe. Period!

Why did our perception evolve to keep us safe? Back in the early days of our existence, the world was a very dangerous place and predators were, quite literally, lurking around every corner. In order to survive, we had to adapt to our environment. We had to learn to process information very quickly or we would fall prey to one of those predators and most certainly die.

In other words, if we had to take the time to question whether or not something in the bushes was a predator, we were already dead. That is where perception came into play. We evolved and learned to map our environment so our mind could use that information to make the split-second decisions we needed to survive.

Perception uses fear of the unknown to keep you safe. Your programming is telling you to avoid anything new or unfamiliar. Taking risks and action can be a challenging and scary proposition.

If you saw the children's movie *The Croods*, you may recall that whenever the main character, Grug, told his family about the past, it always ended the same way: "tried something new and died."

Even when we think we are in control of our fears, our need for safety will be prioritized over everything else.

Let's break it down. Our minds evolved to use assumptions to place meaning on our lives. This served us well when we were cavemen, but how does it play out in the modern world? It certainly comes in handy when we drive. Imagine hurtling down the freeway at 80 mph without using assumptions to process information very quickly! But how does it work for things like creativity, relationships, or taking risks to reach goals? Not so well, unfortunately.

To understand how big the challenge can be, we first need to understand that there are three key things that dictate how we create our lives. Our ability to:

- Recognize opportunities

- Make decisions

- Take action

This creates a problem because our perception evolved to do the opposite of these three things.

Assumptions severely limit your ability to see opportunities. Since your perception evolved to assess risk very quickly, you often do not take time to see anything new or see creatively. In order to see an opportunity not evident at first sight, you have to allow your mind to assess the situation fully. Again, your perception is looking for threats, not opportunities. The program your mind is using to process information is outdated and severely limits your ability to see opportunity.

That is only part of the problem. Once again, perception can also impact your ability to make a good decision. Your assumptions are based on your beliefs. What happens when the beliefs fueling your assumptions are inaccurate? Think about it this way. Remember the example of the Google search? It probably doesn't shock you to hear that not all of the information on the internet is 100 percent accurate. Neither is all the information from your past. As a result, the meaning you place on your current experience is also inaccurate. It is very difficult to make a good decision with bad information.

Perception also makes taking action very difficult. Since your perception's job is to keep you safe, your mind is programmed to tell you to avoid doing anything new or unfamiliar. Uncharted territory may be unsafe, and your perception hates anything it cannot control. The fear of uncertainty is one of the reasons why change is so hard.

Perception uses assumptions to give meaning to your experiences, and your life becomes a pattern with your past casting a shadow over your future. Your past predicts your future and you get caught in a loop, a perception loop. Having a successful life depends on your ability to break free of these patterns. This is hard to do when you do not even know the pattern exists in the first place.

Here is how it works. Every day you have experiences, and your perception places meaning on those experiences. Your perception searches your memory for the experience most similar to the one you're having now and applies the same meaning it did the last time. When you have the same meaning, you do the only logical thing and make the same decision.

That is how the pattern repeats in your life—lather, rinse, repeat—because, as stated previously, your past is always casting a shadow over your future. Welcome to the Matrix!

An analogy to explain perception is to compare it to a video game app on your smartphone. When you play a video game, you are inserting yourself into a virtual world. You understand that everything you see is not real and what is displayed on the screen is nothing more than a program, which was designed to keep you engaged and playing.

Everything you are seeing and experiencing in this game is dictated by the program. The game interacts with you through a process of if/then statements. If the player does this, then the game reacts by doing that, and so on for the entire game. Without this in the program, it would be a bunch of useless lines of code.

Your perception works on the same principle as the if/then statement. When you have an experience, your perception uses the same if/then process to assign meaning to that experience. If this happens to me, then it means that. In life, just like in the game, your experiences are meaningless to you until your perception kicks in and attaches meaning to them.

One of perception's other primary jobs is to establish intent. Does this person intend to cause me harm? Does this situation pose a risk for me? Perception assigns intent to our experience in microseconds. When we perceive someone's intent is to harm us, we get thrown into fear. It doesn't matter if the danger is real or imaginary, physical or emotional. We are very rarely in danger and because of this, the vast majority of our fear is imaginary. This imagined fear causes most of our emotional pain and suffering.

EMOTIONS: GIFT OR CURSE? WHAT DO THEY MEAN, ANYWAY?

It's often said your greatest gift is also your greatest weakness. This statement perfectly describes your emotions. Emotions are your greatest gift, but, if you misunderstand their meaning or have never been taught how to process them, they can hold you back and undermine you more than any other factor. Emotions often become a source of drama when they should be our greatest teachers.

It's mind-blowing to realize, as a general rule, that we as humans have not taken the time to understand our emotions. It's sad to think how few people know how to understand or deal with emotions, when emotions play such a critical role in our lives. Humanity's relationship with emotions is more dysfunctional than any other aspect of life, which is really saying something.

When we started digging to better understand our emotions, we were amazed at how little information is out there explaining them. A negative emotion, as it relates specifically to our interactions with others, means we perceive somebody has crossed a boundary. That's it, and it's really just that simple . . . until it's not.

Here are the three types of boundaries:

- Personal physical boundary

- Emotional boundary

- Property boundary

The first one is pretty simple. It deals with your physical body. Anytime someone or something makes unwanted physical contact with you, you have a negative emotional response in order to protect yourself. The third one is also simple. When somebody takes something that belongs to you, you get angry. You protect what you believe is yours because these are the things you think you need in order to survive.

The second one, the emotional boundary, is where things seem to get really complicated. You determine whether or not someone has crossed an emotional boundary entirely through your perception of the situation. Not only that, emotional boundaries are vastly different according to background and culture and there are no clear-cut rules as to what an emotional boundary is.

We are not just taking in the words someone says, we are also evaluating things like body language, the tone of their voice, and lots of other factors. Everything can go off the rails quickly if we are not careful in our responses.

The other thing that makes it hard is that we are invested in what we believe to be true. We are less concerned with facts than we should be. This is one more way evolution is kicking us in the ass. Have you ever heard the term confirmation bias? It is defined as the tendency to search for, interpret, favor, and recall information in a way that confirms your preexisting beliefs. Why would you do that? It seems very counterintuitive, doesn't it?

From an evolutionary standpoint, you do this for several reasons. Remember that your biggest source of fear is rejection. You hate to be wrong because you fear rejection. Rejection reinforces the idea you are not good enough. The second evolutionary reason is, when our ancestors were fighting for their lives, one misstep meant they were dead. This psychological component brings up fear to let you know when you need to reevaluate your current thinking, so you do not make that same mistake twice.

This means, deep inside of you, being wrong equals death. You need to have confidence that the meaning you place in an experience is true, because you instinctively know your survival depends on that information being correct. You become defensive about it because there is so much at stake. Of course, there is not as much at stake as we believe. It is our survival programming pulling us in the wrong direction.

That does not even count how much success in our society depends on being right. This is especially true in childhood. When you are right, you get an A, and all the loving praise, validation, and awards that go along with it. If you are wrong, you get an F, and all the accompanying rejection and admonishment of being a failure.

There's also another reason. Your perception is based on the past, which means you might not think you are wrong when you perceive that someone said something to hurt you. This is because if someone in the past used the same words the current person is using, and in the past those words were used to hurt you, then those words still mean something similar to you even though on their own they have no negative meaning. You might recall a situation when you said something to someone and they went ballistic on you for no apparent reason. You were left scratching your head, only to find out later that you inadvertently used a word that had caused them pain in the past.

There is still more to this piece of the perception puzzle. The last part is the most complicated and mind-bending. If you can only see and perceive what you believe is possible, your mind is only looking for information it believes to be possible. After all, why would it waste time looking for things it doesn't believe are possible? This is why people can have such different interpretations of the same situation. Have you ever had a misunderstanding with someone and, when you started comparing your interpretations, the two were not even close?

That is when things get even more emotionally charged, because you start questioning the other person's intentions. This makes you feel crazy, or think the other person is crazy. Have you noticed in these types of situations that the other person is often stuck on one single point of the conversation and seems to miss everything else you said? In fact, they did not hear anything else you said, they only heard the one point they are stuck on.

Let us explain. They did hear the words, but their perception blocked out the parts of the conversation not in alignment with their beliefs. They only focused on the part of the conversation congruent with what they believed. This is true because, again, their perception only puts importance on those things that they believe are possible. The part of the interaction that seems to be missing is, in fact, missing because of perception limiting them in what they retain. The good news is neither of you are crazy. You are just working off different information and making different assumptions of meaning. This is happening on both sides of the conversation; you are guilty of doing the same.

THE EMOTIONAL BLAME GAME: YOU ONLY WIN WHEN YOU LOSE

The biggest challenge we face in this area is that we are constantly making our emotions about other people and their emotions about us. The real power of our emotions is not when they tell us that something is wrong on the outside; it is when they tell us there is something wrong on the inside.

Ask yourself this question: Why is it that when someone gets angry because they assumed the worst about you, you are the one who is expected to apologize?

Notice how this concept plays out in a conversation. Let's say you are talking with your partner and you realize something you said upset them. You ask what is wrong and they explain how what you just said offended them. You ask them what they think you meant by what you just said. After they respond, you explain it was not what you meant at all and that you meant them no harm. This explanation, with the possible acknowledgment of a poor delivery, should be the end of the conversation, right? Wrong! We all know damn well that is never truly the end of that conversation. Do you ever wonder why?

It revolves around everything we have been talking about in this chapter. Here is the worst part: Who almost always ends up apologizing in this conversation? It is likely you, even if only to make peace. Here is where things get tricky. Someone made an assumption about your intent in making the comment you made. Were you intending to disrespect the person, or do them harm in any way?

For the sake of this discussion let's say no, as that's most often the case in these types of situations. This is ironic because, if you now apologize for insulting or disrespecting them, you actually end up inflicting harm on them and on yourself. Say what? Right, it's confusing, but here is how it works. The biggest benefit your emotions provide is being your clearest indicator that you're dealing with a false piece of information floating around in your subconscious mind, wreaking havoc on your life. Your negative emotions are there to protect you by telling you when someone has crossed an emotional boundary. But what does it mean when you mis-interpret the situation and a boundary was not crossed? It means a false belief caused you to misinterpret the situation.

When you are able to recognize you got the interpretation wrong, you can follow that mistake back to the belief, allowing you the opportunity to question a limiting belief that you hold to be true. This also gives you some insights into your subconscious mind and belief system, which is invaluable information and sometimes hard to come by.

Back to the earlier conversation. When you apologize for hurting someone after they misinterpret what you said, you are simultaneously robbing them of a chance to question a belief that holds them back and reinforcing that belief, making it stronger. You make yourself weaker whenever you do not speak your truth.

Let's dive into this a little deeper. Have you ever wondered why the things that make you mad affect you this way? Why do some things con-tinually trigger your anger? If one issue seems to keep coming up for you, then it more than likely has to do with a misinterpretation on your side, and not from the other people in your life. This means you hold a false belief in that area.

For instance, because of James's childhood, he was overly sensitive anytime he perceived that someone was calling him stupid. They did not necessarily have to say the word *stupid*. Anytime someone would say something that even suggested he was dumb, he would freak out. This was a huge emotional trigger because of his kindergarten experiences.

Had James been able to properly assess what was going on, he could have followed his negative emotional reactions back to the belief he was still harboring from childhood about his level of intelligence. Once he eventually did, we discovered these principles, but he went through years of unnecessary anguish and blame because he misunderstood the mea-ning of his emotions.

The bottom line is we live in a society that celebrates being right and demonizes being wrong. We have the whole thing backward. We need to celebrate the discovery of being wrong, because life was never about fin-ding answers; it's about asking the right questions.

Finding answers is easy, asking the right questions is the challen-ging part. It is only when you are willing to be wrong about your interpretations that you can shift and grow. Being right all the time will keep you stuck forever.

That conversation we talked about might seem trivial. However, if you fully understand the impact of the concepts described within it, that conversation can change your life. Those of us who summon the courage to question everything, every interpretation, and everything we hold true, are the ones who have the opportunity to be the happiest and have the most impact on the world around us.

Your emotions are the key to your freedom if you learn to understand how they work, what they mean, and how to process them. Your emotions are the only window that you have into your subconscious mind. Most people are constantly slamming that window shut out of fear before they even get to peek inside.

PLEASE GOD, MAKE IT STOP

The vast majority of your negative emotions have to do with a misinterpretation of self. Most of this book is designed to help you change this. There is one more form of negative emotion that is worth covering in this section because it has become an epidemic in our society: Anxiety.

What is the source of most anxiety? We associate it most with misplaced expectations or trying to place conditions on uncertainty. We are constantly trying to predict what is going to happen. When we are wrong it fuels anxiety. Every time things don't turn out the way we thought it would, we think that we are failing or something bad is going to happen. This is not necessarily our fault, as this is how our minds evolved to work. Our survival was based on our ability to predict what was going to happen next. That is why our mind is always trying to move us toward things it can control (toward certainty) because it believes those things are safe. Growth, however, is all about moving into uncertainty, which is by definition the unknown. Here is the really ironic part: The more you try to move your life forward, the more uncertainty you are engaging in, which means you also have the most opportunity for anxiety. This is why most people choose not to go after their dreams and fail to change. When they are offered a choice, they choose to move toward certainty—not away from it.

How do you move past the anxiety? The simple answer is that you have to stop placing expectations on uncertainty. Unfortunately, that is not as easy as it sounds, because your mind simply does not work that way. For millions of years the human mind's main job was to gather all the available information to predict what was going to happen next. The human mind has literally evolved to be a probability calculator. That being said, with awareness of how your mind works, you can learn to become less invested in your predictions or interpretations of things. If you tell yourself going into any given situation that you are probably going to be wrong about how things will unfold, you will be way less affected by the results. You can even get to where you start getting excited about the fact that you were right in your prediction about being wrong. If you adopt the belief that your prediction of a given situation will almost certainly miss the mark, then you will almost always be right.

This is why beliefs like, "Everything that happens is in my best interest," can be so powerful. The trivial little things we tell ourselves when things aren't going as expected can be very powerful hacks to subdue anxiety and keep us moving forward with an open, positive frame of mind. The key that is often missed is figuring out why things didn't go as we expected. We have to learn from our results. We have to look at the situation and ask why things turned out the way they did. This is how you map your way forward.

Here is a story to help illustrate the point. Whenever a new entrepreneur asks James for business advice, he tells them that in order to achieve anything, you must first believe it's possible. You have to foster this belief, which always starts with getting clarity about what you want to create and, most importantly, why you want to create it. Once you have the "what" and the "why," you have to construct a narrative around the "how." On some level this narrative must be believable. It starts with a simple mapping exercise. What are the steps I need to take? What are the things that need to happen for me to go from where I am now to the outcome I want to achieve? Whatever the plan that you're constructing, it must be based on believable scenarios. In other words, it can't all be "perfect world" ideas. For example, if you are trying to go from one to a hundred, you don't just assume you will be able to get there in increments of 10 all the way up; you have to make it reasonable. Once you get to the end of this exercise, you should walk away with the belief that what you are trying to create is in fact possible. Here is the most important step:

Once you finish and you fully believe it is possible, you need to throw all that work away and completely detach from that particular path forward. It will never work out exactly that way—and this is where most people fall down. They have tied what they think success looks like to that particular plan. They get overly invested in it proceeding that way, so when it doesn't, they believe they are failing. They try to force things to be a certain way, which often severely limits their experience and possibilities, often killing their dream. When you spend your time being excited about all the new possibilities that life is presenting to you, rather than focusing on how things are different than you expected them to be, you will be happier and more fulfilled.

GLUING THE PIECES BACK TOGETHER

STORIES

Steph: *Where Do I Go from Here?*

The morning after my suicide attempt in the hotel, I woke up on the shower floor and I was untied. To this day I have no idea how that happened. There was no way I could have ever reached up and removed the rope myself. All the doors to the room were still locked. I kept thinking, "Did someone come in here and untie me?" I was so confused.

I stood up and looked in the mirror. I had deep gashes and bruises on my neck and was shocked at how bad I looked. I felt a lot of emotion, wondering why I was still there. How could I still be alive? I started crying.

I sat on the bed and debated whether I should just do it again. I was already there in the hotel. Maybe the rope just came undone? Maybe I should try again? I thought of other ways I could do it, but I also felt shame because I couldn't do anything right, not even kill myself.

Finally, I thought, maybe I will just pack up my stuff and go to my mom's and see what happens next with my life. It was a long drive, and I kept asking myself, *Why did I live? Why am I still here? How was I untied?*

What does this all mean? I really didn't understand what had happened, and I was still in shock.

When I got to my mom's house, she took one look at me and immediately knew. She straight up asked me, "Why did you do that?" She was crying. I said, "because I don't want to be here anymore."

I proceeded to tell her the story of what happened and how I didn't know how I got untied. I didn't know how I survived. She looked at me and said, "The reason you are still alive is because you have a purpose here and you need to find out what that means."

I felt shocked by her response. A purpose? Everything up until that point in my life had been awful, every bit of it. How could I have a purpose here? Because of all my sadness and depression, a purpose had never even dawned on me.

I thought a lot about what my mom said to me. I thought maybe I did belong here after all. My internal dialogue really started to change after that. That's when I decided to put the idea of suicide on hold and give life another chance.

If I was going to survive, I would need to find something to be positive about. I didn't feel like I had a lot of love in the world. I thought I would start by rebuilding the relationship with my mother. I hoped deep inside that she still loved me. I had never really told anyone who I really was. I felt like if they knew the real me, they wouldn't want anything to do with me. That's why I shut her out. I just wanted love, and I was finally open to experiencing that. Today we are good friends and I am very grateful for that relationship.

James: *No Way Out*

When I got to jail I had no idea how long I was going to be there. The weight of that uncertainty was crushing. For the first time in my life, I was depressed, and I mean really depressed. I just slept and kept sleeping until I couldn't sleep anymore. When I finally got up, I had to really question where I would go from there. Was I going to be able to get through this alive?

Those jail units are a scary place. A lot of the inmates couldn't handle the pressure, and a few of them attempted suicide while I was there, with at least one succeeding.

Here I was, in a box, literally forgotten about, feeling like nobody cared about me. The absolute worst part was being alone. I was alone with the very person I was most afraid of being alone with, myself. I had to either come to terms with the person I had become or kill myself.

During the three months when I had been on the run, a good friend helped me to get sober. When the law finally caught up with me and took me back to jail, I was clean and sober, which was the best thing that could have happened to me.

Being in solitary meant that I only got out of my cell for one hour every other day. I was stuck in my cell alone with nothing to do. I began to write letters like crazy to everyone I could think of. I was desperate for contact with the outside world. My mom couldn't afford to take my collect calls, and my dad was too cheap. I wrote to family members and friends. I must have written a hundred letters. Every day I would wait for the mail, wondering if anyone was thinking about me. There was a guy that would go cell to cell delivering the mail and sure enough, no mail for me. Every day, no mail. Why would anyone write me back? I felt abandoned, alienated, and forgotten.

Finally, one day, I got a letter from my father. I was pretty disappointed at first because the letter was a single, simple paragraph. He gave me this piece of advice: "As we become adults it becomes very difficult for us to take any time away from our life to learn, or to improve ourselves. I don't know how long you're going to be stuck in there, but don't let that time go to waste."

My dad had long since straightened out his life and become a good man. I had never considered him to be a very spiritual or intuitive person, but that piece of advice helped me decide how I was going to spend my time while I was locked up. I knew I needed something to do. I couldn't sit there and worry a second longer.

My biggest curse, being thrown into solitary confinement, turned out to be my greatest gift. I decided I was going to learn, live, and improve myself, whatever it looked like. I was going to make it to the other side.

With a desire to live and better myself, I knew I needed to get information. I started reading every book I could get my hands on. At first, it was mostly spiritual, meditation, and self-help books, so I could learn everything I could about myself.

My reading skills were poor, and sometimes I would have to ask the guards about certain words in the books I was reading. Over time my reading ability improved dramatically. I also started doing pushups and sit-ups. I tried to do a lot of meditating. My attitude was, "What have I got to lose? I might as well try." I wrote so many letters that I began to improve my handwriting, which had previously been barely legible. I also became better at spelling.

The particular spiritual book that had the biggest impact on me was *Be Here Now*, by Ram Das. I read it several times. What intrigued me about that book was the idea that there was more to understand about life. It opened me up to the idea that the way I perceived the world wasn't the only way. It helped me see that I was capable of understanding more. I sensed that there was something else I was missing. The internal world Ram Das described was much bigger than the external world I lived in.

I would call the jail psychologist down to talk to me and have conversations about what I was reading. She finally told me, "Look, nothing is wrong with you. I can't come down here and talk to you anymore. I'm not here to shoot the shit with people who are not mentally ill."

My thirst for learning became stronger and stronger. I wanted to learn about what had gone wrong. I wanted to learn about myself. One of the things I figured out from reading those books was that I didn't feel safe. If I was going to move forward, I had to find a way to feel safe inside myself.

Ironically, that jail cell became a safe haven for me. Yes, I was alone and the food was shitty, but I got three meals a day. I started to use my situation as a place for healing. Meditation became a tool I could rely on to ground myself and get to a good place. The uncertainty of everything going on around me would set in, and I would wonder about what was going to happen to me, how long I would remain locked up. I was being held while awaiting court appearances, a process that could take anywhere from six months to two years.

I began using affirmations. I would tell myself, over and over, "I am safe. I am safe. Everything is going to work out. Everything is going to work out. I am safe." I told that to myself as many times as it took in order for the anxiety I felt about my situation to subside. Meditation and affirmations became my best friends. I started to feel free inside that box, which was nothing I had ever felt before.

One of the things I realized was, if I was going to change, I needed to figure out how to become positive again. In my decline, I had lost any sense of optimism and positivity. My view of the world had become very dark. I knew from the books I read that it was crucial to shift my thinking from the negative to the positive. Even when I did that, I always jumped to the most negative aspects of my thoughts, and the most negative conclusions about what was going to happen to me.

As part of trying to cope with where I was and the uncertainty of my future, I started building this positive picture in my mind. Every piece of information I read about my case and about the judge I would look at from the most positive perspective. From that point forward, I really started looking for the positive in everything.

Making that shift to positive made all the difference. Not only in being in jail and that experience, but in moving forward with my life. If there are positives in any situation, I was going to find them, identify with them, and focus on them.

Steph: *What the Hell Was I Thinking?*

Even though my life has been hard, I have always considered myself to be a dreamer. I knew in my heart that I was capable of more, though I had never ventured out to pursue my dreams.

One day I was sitting on my couch thinking about my life. The thought came to me, *If I can choose my life, why aren't I choosing differently?* I wondered what my life could look like. I was tired of all the suffering. I was tired of all the sadness.

If I had a purpose, I needed to try and figure it out, not just hope that it would simply land in my lap. I started writing down all my dreams, goals, and everything I thought I deserved in life. As it hit me that I deserved more, I realized I deserved happiness. This was the first time I thought I could be alone and be okay with it. I knew I could figure out a way to be happy. From that day forward, I was determined to figure it out. I wrote down everything I wanted to become, the sort of person I wanted to be, the people I wanted to attract into my life, and everything I wanted to do in the future. I even described everything I wanted in a future partner.

As I shifted my mindset, I realized that I was bigger than all this sadness, pain, suffering, and anger. I realized this was all just a negative story I was telling myself and it was ruining me. I was ready to break free of all the darkness and move into the light.

James: *Taking My Power Back*

One of the things I had to deal with while I was in jail was an idea that my mom had planted deep in my brain. The idea that the world is a cruel place, and people are out to get you. The only model I had for the concept of forgiveness was the one I had learned in church.

In my cell, I wrote long lists of all the people I resented for harming me and I tried to find forgiveness for them: the teacher who had humiliated me, the bullies that had hurt me, the people who were supposed to be my friends but backstabbed me, the friends who cheated on me with my girlfriends, all the shitty women I had been with. None of this made sense to me. I had treated these people with kindness and generosity, and it felt like all I got in return was a kick in the face.

Slowly I realized it wasn't my kindergarten teacher's abuse that caused me to feel shitty about myself. It was my interpretation of that abuse that caused me to feel the way I did.

I would read through and meditate on these lists. What if I could bring myself to become grateful for all these people? What would that look like? Or maybe I should go through the list and forgive these people.

As I was going through and offering meditations and prayers of forgiveness for those on the list, something didn't feel right. One day, as I was reading through my list, I had an epiphany. I was looking down at it and thought to myself, *The only common denominator in all those situations was me. What if all this is my fault? What if I somehow created all these situations in my life?*

I began to think through the ramifications of what I was saying. Was I the creator of all my experiences? It didn't make sense that you could create some things and not others. Either I created all of it, or I created none of it. What did that mean to me?

If I was the creator of my experiences, then I was responsible for all the shitty things that had ever happened to me. If I wasn't the creator of my experiences, then it meant that none of it was my fault, and the world really was a shitty place that I didn't want to play the game of life in anymore.

As I evaluated those two options, I thought about what adopting one of them meant to me. If I decided I wasn't the creator, that things really were happening to me based on random circumstances, and the world really was a shitty place, then I didn't want to be here anymore. I had gotten the shit kicked out of me enough. What if all this really was somehow my fault, what did that mean? It meant I would have to take responsibility for everything. Based on how shitty my life was, that was a lot of responsibility to take on.

When I looked over that list again, I realized it was, in fact, all me. I decided I was the creator of my experiences. I was going to figure out the mechanism by which I created my life. It was on that day that I took full responsibility for all my experiences. I decided I was going to create a new life beyond anything I ever imagined possible.

This is where my journey started. I came to understand much later that by having this realization, or epiphany, I was rejecting the concept of powerlessness and was taking my power back for the first time in my life. That was the turning point for me.

Steph: *Having Anxiety Over My Anxiety*

I have anxiety. When I was in my early twenties, a friend called me up and told me she had been in a fight with her boyfriend. She was so upset she had to pull her car over and breathe into a paper bag. Her anxiety attacks were so bad she had to do this to make herself calm down. I felt bad for her, but I didn't fully understand what anxiety entailed.

When I realized that I had anxiety, I noticed that it showed up much differently for me. I have always been an obsessive worrier, and I just thought everyone was the same way. I had adopted this as part of my childhood trauma. This anxiety led to intense bouts of anger. When I get angry, I do not lash out, I shut down, and I shut people out. If I stay there too long, things get very dark for me, and all I see is negativity and sadness.

I did some research about anxiety and how to overcome it. I discovered that forty million people suffer from this! Why do so many of us suffer from anxiety?

For me, it always comes down to worrying about my children's safety and what other people think. I will always care about my children's safety and where they are, no matter what. Likewise, caring about what other people think is a never-ending battle. So many of us walk around caring about what other people think of us. Guess what they are worrying about? What we think about them!

I had to decide what things meant the most to me and how I was going to grow through this. For me, my choices were to choose to love and accept myself for everything that I am, or to judge myself for everything I am not. I choose happiness over worry, realizing that nobody is perfect. We are all doing the best we can with the tools we have available to us. I have vowed to release these negative thoughts as they come up, because worrying robs my life of joy.

James: *Judgment Day*

As I started to move forward, I realized if I decided to take my power back, I was then responsible for everything that would happen to me. Except the next thing that was going to happen to me would be decided by the judge ... so in a way, I was still struggling with this idea of powerlessness.

Finally, I had my day in court. I pleaded guilty to the charges and then had to wait for my sentencing hearing, which happened a few weeks later. Before I was sentenced, I wrote a letter to the judge. It wasn't long, less than a page. I just wanted to get across one point.

"Your Honor," I wrote, "I want you to know that I take 100 percent responsibility for all my actions. And whatever punishment you deem appropriate, I will gladly accept." I wrote about my sobriety, and my dreams for when I got out, but the whole point of the letter was that I did it, it was my fault, nobody else was responsible for all that had happened.

When I finally did have my day in court, the judge openly recognized my letter and commented on what a rare thing it was for him to have somebody come into his courtroom and take full responsibility. He gave me six more months in jail. I had been facing up to six years in prison, and I got six months in jail.

After it was all said and done, I served fifteen months in that box. As I look back, I couldn't be more grateful for the time spent there. Even though I had been locked in a box, for the first time in my life I was free. I felt liberated in that cell and discovered a version of myself I never knew existed. I was thankful for every second I spent there. But Lord knows, I don't think I could do it again.

When I was scheduled to get out, there was a hold put on my release. Nobody told me why. I sat there for three more weeks. Then I got shipped off to the state of Nevada and ended up in jail there awaiting trial again. All this was because I had been stupid enough to commit crimes in more than one state. About two weeks after I arrived there, I got a call telling me I was getting out. My heart sank into my stomach. I immediately broke out into a cold sweat. I walked over to the toilet and puked. I was in middle-of-nowhere Nevada, with thirty dollars to my name, and no idea what I was going to do or where I was going to go.

I walked down to the local Greyhound bus station and bought a ticket back home. There were a couple of court mandated things I had to do, such as complete a drug rehab program and check in for probation. But I was free and scared.

I knew what I wanted to do, and I had a bunch of new ideas. I was so afraid that I was going to fail, that my life would go back to the way it was, and I would either end up in prison or dead.

It was really hard to assimilate back into society. During the first few months out, there were a lot of starts and stops. I would re-engage with life, start working again, and then pull back. It took me a full year to get to a point where I was comfortable enough to start implementing my plan to change my life and figure out how to create something greater for myself.

Steph: *I Got This*

After I realized that I wanted more, and deserved more, it still took me nine months to leave the relationship I was in, because I was scared. It wasn't an abusive relationship, but it wasn't a loving relationship either. For the first time ever, my own happiness was more important to me than keeping someone else happy.

When I finally left, I was surprised at how easy it was, and how wonderful it felt. Before, I would have cared more about the other person's feelings than my own, and whether or not they would hate me for leaving them.

Still, starting over was so unbelievably hard. I didn't know what I was going to do with my life. I didn't know what it would be like to be alone. I think everyone is scared of the unknown. The truth is, even bad relationships feel comfortable because they are familiar. Like they say, misery loves company.

I slowly started to rebuild my life. I wanted to be comfortable in my own skin. As I started to move forward, my self-confidence began to grow. My eyes started to open up to my potential for growth and becoming more. I put my own needs first for the first time in my life.

After all the years of abuse, all the sadness, and all the self-hate, I was finally okay with myself. I was finally okay with being alone. I finally felt that I didn't need a man in my life to love me. I finally began to love myself. The better I felt about myself, the less I cared about what other people thought.

And then, of course, I met someone.

TWO LOST SOULS: THE LIGHT AT THE END OF THE TUNNEL

STORIES

Steph: *Green eyes, are you holding the door for me?*

I was finally at a point in my life where I didn't need or want a man. I was actually okay with myself, being alone, and not worrying about finding someone to love me. I was content with my life. I had an office job downtown, and I tried to keep busy.

One sunny spring day I was walking back from lunch. As I approached my building (at least 100 feet away), I saw a man standing there, holding the door open. I wondered why he was just standing there holding the door. I was expecting other people to walk in before me. I walked in the door and said, "Thank you," and he walked in after me. I realized that he had been holding the door for me!

I blushed after realizing that he had been watching me walk through the parking lot and then had held the door open. He said that he worked on the first floor. As I walked into the elevator, I told him I worked on the third floor and I stuck my hand out, saying, "My name is Steph," to which he replied, "My name is James."

As I rode up the elevator, I said to myself, *He is very handsome and seems nice, but I can't date anyone.* I began wondering why I believed that a guy couldn't just be a gentleman without the expectation of dating. I stopped myself in my own tracks and decided to just end the conversation in my head.

Exactly one week later, on a Wednesday, I was leaving work and I saw James get out of a coworker's truck and start walking toward the building. Though we spotted each other, he didn't think I could see him. He wanted to be on the same trajectory as I was, so he started walking between the cars and ducking down to make it look like he was just going to run into me. He walked over to my car and struck up a conversation. I acted like I hadn't just seen his parking-lot ninja moves (to this day he denies that I saw him do that). I could tell that he was extremely nervous but he seemed very kind. I thought to myself, as I looked into his incredible green eyes, those eyes could get me into some trouble. But I agreed to have lunch with him sometime.

The very next day, I was busy in my office and telling my coworker about the guy I met who worked downstairs. As I was talking about him, he walked right into my office. I probably looked like a deer in the headlights! My face flushed, and I jumped up to talk to him.

He said, "You ready to have that lunch?"

I replied, "How about in an hour?" Thinking to myself, shit, couldn't he have given me some warning? He just comes into my office at eleven o'clock in the morning wanting to eat. I don't even know this guy! I became very nervous knowing I had a date in an hour. I had told myself I didn't want to date, I didn't need to date, and I definitely didn't need or want a man in my life. I needed more alone time; I was freaking out.

I decided to go anyway. If he had enough guts to just waltz his way into my office, maybe one lunch couldn't hurt.

James: *Déjà vu, and I don't even know you*

That day in the parking lot with Steph, my God, it was an experience like I had never felt before. I started talking to her, and the entire world around us froze. It just froze. It was a sunny day, and she was the most beautiful woman I had ever seen. I said the stupidest, most ridiculous things, and they just kept flying out of my mouth. I said to myself, What the hell is wrong with you? I was so nervous, and I didn't want to stop talking to her, so I just said whatever came to my head. Verbal vomit, and it wasn't good.

I asked her if she eats! Oh my hell, of course she eats! She laughed and replied, "Yeah, I eat." I asked her if she would eat with me. It just kept getting worse for me, but she was laughing. At that moment, the sun hit her face, and I melted right then and there. She has the biggest, most incredible smile. The kind that makes all of your worries melt, and I knew I was finished. I had the most overwhelming feeling that I had known this girl my whole existence, not my life, my entire existence. I knew she was the one for me.

Steph: *Another loser? But wait, there's more*

It was now Sunday evening. James and I had gone out every single day since our lunch date on Thursday. He opened my eyes to life, the world, and made me question if there was more. Is this real? Is he really this kind, loving person that I had been longing for my whole life?

We were out on a Sunday drive and he told me we had to talk. I pulled into a store parking lot and he told me his entire story, all of it. Tears were streaming down my face as I wondered if I could date someone who had been in jail. I just stood there outside my car, in deep shock. He hugged me and told me he wanted more for his life. He looked deep into my eyes and told me he was done. He was done having such a shitty life. He was done being so sad. He was clean and wasn't going to look back.

I looked into those eyes of his and, somehow, I knew he was telling the truth. I asked him why he was telling me this, that he didn't owe me anything as we had only just met a few days ago. He replied, "I feel so connected to you and it wouldn't be fair if I started this relationship off with lies. I don't want you to find out later and have you resent me."

I couldn't believe the level of vulnerability he was sharing with me. I had never met anyone that willing to share their story, knowing at any moment I could have rejected him. I could have said this was too much, that I didn't want to sign up for it. He was so broken, yet so was I. The only difference was that he shared his story, while I still had mine buried deep inside. I wondered how people had the courage to share their story with others and if I could find that same courage to share mine.

James: *Love at first sight . . . awkward*

Jail was, of course, an awful place to be, but I convinced myself I needed the alone time. I needed to be free of drugs and the life I had been living.

I constantly thought about rebuilding my life and how I would do that. For the first time in a very long time, I had dreams and goals. I wasn't going to go back to my shitty life. I was going to be wildly successful. I didn't know how, but I wasn't going to give up.

I didn't think about dating. That was something I wasn't prepared for, and all I had ever had were heartaches with women. Though I always wanted a deep connection with someone, it just wasn't top on my list of priorities. I needed to be the type of man who would deserve to be with an amazing woman before I went looking for a relationship.

Just over a year after getting out, I met Steph, and that all changed. I shared my story with her, and she stayed. I couldn't believe it. I had nothing, not one thing to my name, and she stayed. She wasn't looking for "things," she was looking for someone who was real, but also someone who had a heart, and a dream. I had both.

After one week, I told her that I loved her. She replied with a sort of laughing "Thank you." After two weeks, she told me that she loved me, too.

We were both broken human beings who wanted more out of life. We had both hit rock bottom, but we were both on our way up. We made an agreement that we would build a great life together and stop at nothing in our pursuit of happiness. We didn't know what it would look like, but we got married nine months after our first lunch date together.

At the time of our first meeting, I was working a dead-end sales job. Steph helped me open my first email account and showed me how it worked. She put together my first résumé, so that I could apply for other jobs. She helped me build some skills to survive in something other than a restaurant job. She sent out the résumé she had prepared, and that landed me my first job in technology, as a salesman at a computer training facility. This started my very unlikely career in technology.

Steph saw something in me. I had all these ideas, and I was determined to have the greatest comeback of all time. She had been with a lot of losers. The last thing she needed was someone just out of jail and rehab, but she liked the fact that I was full of energy, hope, and enthusiasm. I said I was going to conquer the world. I was going to figure out what it took to be successful.

I sold her on the vision of where I was going, not where I was at. She saw something in my eyes and in my heart and she took a big risk with me. I must have been a good salesperson because when I landed Steph, I made the biggest sale of my life.

CHAPTER
10

WHY IS CHANGE SO HARD?

BLIND SPOTS

One of the keys to the process of growth is finding your blind spots—those things that sit outside your conscious awareness yet hold the keys to unlocking your personal power. These blind spots are not only the challenges you might face, they can also be hidden strengths.

Gaining a clear understanding of not only your weaknesses, but also your strengths, is a crucial part of living up to your full potential. Most successful people spend the vast majority of their time focusing on their strengths, and pay little or no attention to their weaknesses. They stay aware of what they are so they can surround themselves with people who compensate with their own strengths. The challenge most people face is they put all their attention on trying to improve, or better yet hide, their weaknesses because they are so worried about what other people will think of them.

It's been said many times, "You don't know what you don't know," but the opposite is also true; you don't know what you do know. We all have things that come baked into us. Those aspects of self can be both positive and negative attributes. As a matter of fact, the vast majority of our knowledge sits outside our conscious awareness. It is estimated that 95 percent of our cognition is subconscious.

When trying to bring some level of change into our lives, one of the major challenges is that the true issues we are trying to address are deeply hidden in our subconscious mind. This forces us to focus on simply changing behaviors, which is literally attempting to initiate change at the level of effect, not at the level of cause. It is the equivalent of putting a bandage on a wound that is clearly infected and then hoping for the best.

One of the biggest issues facing the personal development space is that people often don't fully understand why they are successful. They take skills or attributes for granted. This is why the old adage "Find someone who is successful and just do what they do," has a very small success record. We tend to listen to people who succeed because we assume they actually know what made them successful. In the vast majority of cases, this simply is not true.

It's not that successful people are trying to mislead you. Many do their best to encourage and help others by explaining what worked for them; but, if they are talking about habits and behaviors, they are missing the most important aspects of change, the aspect of perception. This is why people in the personal development industry keep beating the same old drums. You have to work harder, you have to want it more, you need to be more committed, and you need more urgency. None of this is inherently wrong or bad advice. It might even be something you're missing, but it's based on a very limited view. This type of advice addresses only one small aspect of the necessary personal change process.

There is a lot of talk these days about concepts like mindset and "understanding your why," which are big steps in the right direction because they are perception-based topics. Even though the science shows that having a growth mindset works, there is no explanation for why it works. As a result, we are left to take their word for it. We always want to know why something works, otherwise we will never fully understand the cost of not doing it. In fact, most people fail to realize that there actually is a cost associated with doing nothing. The reason why most everyone's model of change fails, is because they don't measure the true cost of inaction.

Here's how to calculate that cost when you're facing a tough choice that is pushing you to the edge of your comfort zone. Ask yourself, where will you be if you maintain your current behaviors for one week, one month, one year, even ten years? It is very important that you don't lie to yourself in this exercise. It's quite simple really, just basic math. It doesn't matter if you're measuring the cost in pounds, dollars, debt, happiness, physical or mental health, even the quality of your relationships. You are either moving up the scale or down the scale; just calculate the rate of decline and push that number into the future. Remember, from an evolutionary perspective, humans only change when the cost of not changing outweighs the cost of changing. If you lie to yourself about the cost of not changing, which is easy to do, then it is often too late when you wake up to the reality of your situation. Just like our friends who failed to change their habits even after coronary bypass surgery.

Many people seem to believe in "act of God" types of change, hoping someone or something will come in from outside and miraculously make everything better. You are the only one who can disrupt your life and change your path. Stop being shocked by your results! See your life for what it is. The signs are everywhere if you have clarity of perception. Don't be so shocked by illness, divorce, or bankruptcy, because the signs are evident in everything you do.

DOOMED TO FAIL

Change can't be mandated, it must be cultivated.

The statistics for how hard it is to change are alarming and don't seem to be getting any better. In fact, when we started researching them, we didn't believe what we found. Here they are. See for yourself.

- 90 percent of people who try to make changes in their life fail; 90 percent is the average rate of failure straight across the board. With specific things like dieting, the number goes as high as 94 percent. This is not the worst part. The next number is much more disturbing.

- 70 percent of people who manage to change and reach their goal lose everything they achieved, often ending up worse than when they started. This is not just about weight loss, this is everything. For example, 69 percent of second marriages fail.

Do the math. When we look at the percentages, the real success rate of change turns out to be just *3 percent*!

The common mantra is you've got to do the work and want it more than everybody else, but these people did the work. They changed their lives, then lost it all and fell back to where they started. We've experienced this many times during our own journey. James has lost the same 35 pounds seven times in nine years. Seven times! We became obsessed with this problem of why people fail to sustain the changes they make in their lives. It is this question that really leads us back to the discovery of perception and its impact.

We can explain how this works through an all too common story. Imagine a guy walks into the doctor's office and the doctor says, "You are obese, you need to lose weight."

The guy replies, "Why am I obese?"

The doctor says, "Because you eat too much, and you don't exercise."

The guy asks the obvious question, "So what do I need to do to lose weight?"

"You need to eat less and exercise," says the doctor.

That logical advice seems to make sense for the guy, so he does what the doctor advises. He changes his eating habits and starts exercising. It's really hard work, but he sticks with it and loses all the excess weight. He goes back to the doctor's office and the doctor congratulates him. The man goes about his life, but unfortunately, he gains all the weight back in no time flat. He lost the weight and now is right back where he started, or perhaps even worse.

We don't know if you've ever experienced something like that, but we can tell you, it feels super frustrating and self-defeating.

The problem here is that the doctor didn't ask the right question at the very beginning, which was, "What is causing you to eat so much food? What beliefs drive your unhealthy relationship with food?"

This is why the white-knuckle approach to change, the act of forcibly driving yourself in a different direction, doesn't work. The work harder, run faster approach to change only succeeds when you're already going in the right direction—which few people are. It's impossible to change unless you change the underlying belief. If you don't change the belief that is fueling your behavior, the second you stop white knuckling, you shift back to the direction you've always gone.

The rates of failure to maintain change are so high because we've been doing it all wrong. People believe change is all about altering habits. But habits are the effect of the problem, not the source of it. The source of the problem is the belief underneath the habit. If you want to change, you can't just focus on the habits. You must focus on changing the beliefs that are causing the habits in the first place.

The few people who have been able to change and sustain that change somehow changed their underlying beliefs while they were engaged in changing the habit. For the other 70 percent it doesn't work out so well. They are living unconsciously, and suffering the cost of not understanding perception. You can only act in accordance with your beliefs. *The key lesson here is that undertaking change must not only address the undesirable habits, it must also address the beliefs sitting at the core of the behaviors.*

STUCK ON AUTOPILOT

What you believe on the inside is always projected and reflected on the outside. That short statement is a full description of how you perceive your life. Your beliefs become a subconscious pattern, forming a program that will run if you are not putting any attention or focus on that part of your life at any given time. You could compare these belief patterns to habits. They are similar, but a pattern is something that goes much deeper, to the essence of who you are to yourself and others.

All your habits are based on these patterns. These belief patterns drive your autopilot. The question that defines your pattern is, "Where would I end up if I followed the path of least resistance, if I made no conscious effort to direct my behavior in any area of my life?" This is why you can't just wake up one morning and decide that day to do something different, whether it's eat healthy, exercise, wake up early, or be less sad or angry. This is also why it gets very hard to change multiple areas of your life at once; you don't have enough attention to go around.

The challenge you face is being unaware that these patterns exist, and then not knowing how to change any of them. Since they are driven by your perceptions, the beliefs and emotions running the patterns are buried deep in your subconscious mind. Here's an example of how this works. Let's say you decide you want to lose weight, and you put a tremendous amount of effort and time into this process. After a period of time, you accomplish your goal. At that point, you think you have changed the habits and decide you're going to move your focus to another area of your life. You decide to take all that extra time and attention you were putting into losing weight and direct it somewhere else. Seems easy enough, right? Here's the problem: You have no way of knowing if, as a part of your journey to lose weight, you changed the belief pattern that existed underneath the habits.

Now you move your attention to something else. Maybe you focus on your business, or on your relationships. Once you move your conscious attention off one area, your beliefs step in and reset your behavior to match what you really believe inside. You then become a part of that 70 percent. Your weight completely resets to what it was before, or higher than when you started your program. This is the inherent problem with the current model of change. You did what everyone told you to do, you did the work it took to reach your goal, only to have it all ripped away.

This has always been the case with human beings. When we focus on one area of our lives, other areas suffer. We choose among things we want the most, believing we can't have them all. Generally, either we put all our attention into the one thing we want most and allow everything else to remain dysfunctional, or ultimately give up and decide to live out a mediocre existence. Either way, we are not fulfilled or happy.

This is why we emphasize, once more, that we can't just shift behaviors and habits. We must shift at the fundamental level of our beliefs, which means the only true, permanent change comes through a shift in perception.

We all spend much of our existence on autopilot, unconsciously reacting and unconsciously making decisions and taking action. In this book, we are trying to show you not only how to improve the quality of your life, but also how to reprogram your autopilot. By changing the program that is driving your behaviors, you can learn to live consciously.

We are going to give you the script to rewrite that program to better serve you in reaching your goals and dreams, so you can succeed at living a more fulfilling life.

PART FOUR

CRAWLING OUR WAY OUT

THE LONG
WAY HOME

LESS THAN ZERO

When James got out of jail, he was two hundred thousand dollars in debt with felonies on his record. As you can imagine, Steph was less than thrilled about taking on this debt with him, but we were in it together.

He could not get a checking account or a credit card because his credit was completely trashed. The prospects of getting a good-paying job seemed pretty slim. When we say that we started with less than zero, we mean way less.

The sales job James had was paying a couple hundred dollars a week.

Steph had a car and a good job that paid decent money. It was a good start for us.

With the résumé Steph helped him write, James was able to land an interview with a good company who, luckily, didn't do a background check. When he got done with the interview, they offered him the job and asked him to fill out an application for their records. James just about shit himself. He knew there was always a question on those forms about whether you have ever been convicted of a crime, and if you don't answer that question honestly, it is another crime. He also knew that if he answered it correctly, they would rescind the job offer.

In a panic, James excused himself to use the restroom. He was freaking out because it was a good job that would pay more money than he had ever made in his life. James had made a promise to himself that he would never again put himself in a position of compromising his integrity. He also swore to himself he was never going to commit another crime, no matter how small it seemed.

After staying in the bathroom for what seemed like a long time, he came up with a plan. He went out and filled out the application, leaving the "have you ever been convicted of a felony" answer blank. Luckily, that question fell on the back page of the application, and nobody seemed to notice.

It probably helped that James was clean-cut and well-spoken. He didn't raise any warning signs that would cause them to check up on his answers. He got the job, but he always lived in fear of the day when his employer would find out about his past, which they eventually did.

He had been working there for several months when one of the owners of the company called him into his office. James could see that the man seemed agitated. James's job application was sitting on his desk and the website on his computer screen had James's mug shot on it. James's heart dropped. He was thinking, "We were starting to gain some momentum in our lives. We have just gotten married and moved into our own place together. We even managed to put together enough money to get me a car, and now it is going to all come crashing down."

The company owner told James to sit down. "I found out some troubling things about you this morning and I need some answers," he said. James looked at him straight in his eyes and voiced full responsibility for everything. The man looked at the application and said, "You know if you had answered this question correctly, I never would have hired you, and if you had lied, I would have had you arrested!"

James nodded and said, "That is why I did not answer the question. I just wanted a chance to prove myself and to show you I am a good person and a hard worker." It was true, James had been working his ass off. He was well on his way to becoming one of their top performers, and he also had built a solid relationship with the owners.

The owner asked him a lot of questions about the nature of the type of crimes he had committed to make sure James was not a sex offender, a violent criminal, or a risk to any of his other employees. Although the man seemed very frustrated, he also seemed to respect the fact that James was trying to rebuild his life. He said he would do a background check on James, and "if I find you have lied to me, you are out of here." He told James to get back to work.

When James got home and told Steph what had happened, she freaked out, but she was relieved to know he still had his job. This was an experience James would have to relive many times over the years, and every time it would come up, it would really upset Steph, but she always had his back.

It seemed that every time James was climbing the ladder, someone would get jealous of his success, do a little research about his past, and attempt to use the information against him. Not only coworkers, but people James considered to be friends and even a few family members would hang it over his head from time to time.

This didn't bother James too much unless there was a lot on the line. Steph insisted he hire a lawyer to get his record expunged, which he did. That did not seem to help, because once you reach a certain level of success, it's no longer about background checks. When you're being considered for any major role or transaction, they do "due diligence," which is where they dig into every aspect of your life. Most of the time things seemed to work out well, because people seemed to respect the good comeback story, but there were some really awkward conversations.

It once cost us a multimillion-dollar deal, even though James was up front with these people, his record had been expunged, and it had been almost twenty years since he had committed a crime. This was really unsettling at the time, but in the end, because we stayed open, a much better deal came along.

THE HARD WAY

Like we said in the first chapter, when we started this process of personal growth, we had no idea what we were doing. We just made it up as we went along. We had no models for change, and no resources to get one, so we just tried stuff out to see what worked.

When things started moving in the right direction, we kept making adjustments until it worked better. We are still doing the same refining process in our lives today, because this journey is never ending. We based, and continue to base, everything on our experiences and results.

Steph often says that this book and the concepts in it were found through her pain, which is true in many ways. Because James somewhat disassociated from his emotions in his childhood trauma and Steph did not, this journey has been much more emotionally painful for her.

As it pertains to emotional issues, James would often come up with a concept and see if it had any impact on Steph's emotional state. When it came to creating financial success, James would often try to settle in, or get complacent, when he felt like he had hit a ceiling of what was possible for him. This was due to his lack of education, and because he often struggled with his self-confidence in professional situations, because of his beliefs formed in childhood about being stupid.

That is how it went with us. James was always pushing Steph to overcome some type of emotional trauma that was causing her to feel a vast amount of pain. Steph was always challenging James to overcome his false and limiting beliefs, and pushing him way outside his comfort zone.

We found out very quickly that attempting this type of transformation is hard, especially when you don't know what you're doing. If you're not equally committed to that road together, and to each other, it won't work out. We both chose to grow, and though we didn't always grow at the same rate, we would always wait for the other to catch up.

As we started our journey, we simply sat around at night trying to figure out what we believed our issues to be and how to relieve the pain and discomfort we were feeling. We wanted to create a better life for ourselves and our growing family. We needed to identify the issues we had, but this was a tough process. Like most people, we had spent our lives trying to run away from darkness and repressing the emotions associated with it. Now we were trying to name our issues and figure out a way to eradicate them from our lives.

The first issue we identified was that from an early age, we both were made to feel emotionally and physically unsafe. Our childhoods gave us reason to blame others for our pain, which caused us to get very defensive and feel extremely powerless at times. We both grew up in families with early divorces, and our dads caused us to feel a lagging sense of abandonment. James also had a lot of fear around money, growing up in a family that was constantly broke. It was so bad at times that they would go for several months without electricity in their home. The rising cost of living in Southern California at the time forced his family to move 13 times before he finished high school, which meant he had no long-lasting connections or friendships throughout his childhood.

Steph didn't have a lot of trauma regarding money, but she left home at an early age, and this caused the same sense of fear of scarcity. As we would find out later, children growing up often model the behaviors and experiences of their parents. That modeling was not positive for us.

We both believed, to some degree, that we were unlovable because of the abandonment we felt from our fathers and the abuse we experienced as children. Neither one of us felt worthy of love. We felt rejected by life, which made us both feel we weren't good enough and that we had to prove ourselves to the world and to each other.

We both also had self-esteem issues based on our looks. James was insecure about his teeth, which were crooked because his parents could not afford to get him braces. Steph hated her body because of her childhood abuse. James was still fighting a childhood belief that he wasn't smart. We both have respect issues because we felt so disrespected our entire life. We would literally sit down and say to each other, I felt like you didn't respect me, or you were questioning how smart I was. We would realize it was because we both had these issues of worthlessness, abandonment, and insecurity. We probably only made it to this point because we had both stared death right in the eyes and knew what was waiting for us if we didn't push forward.

Another big issue for Steph was that she didn't feel emotionally safe with James, or anyone else for that matter, so she would put her walls up whenever she felt like her belief system was being threatened. She thought being vulnerable was being weak, and that made it hard for her to open up.

Whenever either of us felt like we were being disrespected it made us really angry. When Steph felt threatened, causing her to shut down and shut James out, this made him feel disrespected and that triggered anger. Then he would say something that caused her to feel disrespected. It was a vicious cycle. At times, the journey became very intense for both of us.

To make things worse, we didn't get anywhere emotionally for a very long time. We wasted so much time talking through issues and trying to figure out our false and limiting beliefs, as a consequence of being unwilling to be open and vulnerable with each other. We were literally just going in circles and getting nowhere. It wasn't until we learned how to bring down the walls that we achieved any substantive change in our lives.

This meant not only having to be vulnerable, but also to be willing to be wrong, which was really hard because we are both extremely hard-headed control freaks. What did we have to learn to be wrong about? As it turns out, just about everything. We had to learn how we were wrong concerning ourselves, each other, other people and their intentions, even the world around us.

When immense amounts of stress, pressure, and emotion would come up, as they often did, we had to learn just to stay open to each other and stay open to the possibilities. It took a very long time to learn how to do this, and even to this day, we struggle with it from time to time. When we get stuck it always comes back to this one thing over and over again: One or both of us was not open to the possibility of our current interpretation being wrong, causing us to miss something we needed to know in order to move forward. That is one of the biggest take-aways from this book— your interpretation of any situation is severely limited by on your current information.

As a result of all that, our growth together came kicking and scream-ing. One person growing, the other dragging his or her heels. We were identifying the emotional trends we were seeing. We would look at what triggered our responses. Something would trigger Steph, so she would put her walls back up and stop engaging. For James, he would hold in his anger until it reached the point of spilling out. We started noticing that the level of emotion being displayed wasn't equal to the situations we were experiencing.

We would talk about what triggered these emotional responses. Why did you get so angry when this happened? Why did you get so defensive when this happened? Why did you shut down when this happened? We searched for the source of the emotion or triggers. We would ask each other, "What in me, or you, triggered this reaction that didn't seem to match the circumstances?" It would end up being reactions from beliefs that weren't supported by the facts of our relationship.

For example, because of our abandonment issues, we both felt that at any moment we could be abandoned by the other. Even though there was no sign of that ever happening, that was just how it worked because we used assumptions from our past to place meaning on the present.

It felt like just below the surface of conscious awareness there was a lot of anger for each of us. What triggered our emotions and outbursts?

The source was always based on past experiences, and the things we choose to believe after having lived through those experiences, not the experiences themselves. We never really learned to eradicate those beliefs, though we learned to self-soothe and manage them when they arose. It became a process of learning how to better manage the hands we were dealt, rather than changing those hands. It was not until much later that we discovered we could, in fact, do better than managing the darkness. We did finally learn to change those beliefs, which we will explain in a later chapter.

Over time we started noticing how, once a belief was established, it just started looping around onto itself. Here is an example: When you have an annoyed reaction to something and you don't address that issue by ignoring it, that frustration turns into anger. If you keep ignoring the anger, it can turn to rage. It keeps increasing in intensity until you can't ignore it anymore. Your mind is forcing you to look at the things that cause you pain. If you keep ignoring the issue, the next time that same issue comes up, it comes back stronger and stronger.

Once we managed to follow the emotional distresses back to the underlying belief, we used affirmations and meditations to find relief. Just acknowledging it and bringing it to light made it better. This was the first step in managing the darkness when we couldn't figure out how to eliminate it. Getting better at managing it is enough to shift your perspective to create what you want in life.

The next big issue we both had to deal with was all the resentment we had built up. Even though we had taken responsibility for everything in our past, that did not take away the resentment we felt toward ourselves and everyone we felt had harmed us. The thing about resentment from the past is that it doesn't stay there. It starts dumping all over your life. For us, it was everywhere. To some degree, we resented everyone and everything.

Steph's resentment wasn't so much about other people. She could have blamed anyone and everyone in her past, but she mostly resented herself. She beat herself up. She blamed herself. She had to learn how to be kind and loving to release the resentment. She had to go inside and change her internal dialogue as a way of becoming kind, gentle, and loving to herself.

When you think about resentment and how to release it, using forgiveness usually comes to mind for most people. The traditional models of forgiveness did not resonate for us, because making it all about the other person was still a way of giving them our power. Thus, we decided to change the way we thought about forgiveness entirely.

Instead of us forgiving somebody else for what they did, we accepted that their part in it was none of our business. It became about releasing all the resentment we had toward them. It's important to understand that most abusers, at some point in their lives, were in fact the victim, were not given the love they needed, and were simply trying to express their pain in the only way they know how, by attempting to dominate or control others. Through resentment, we keep the cycle of hate alive. Even if we did not duplicate their actions, any expression of anger generated from that resentment would continue to push that hate into our future, and out into the world.

We know today that forgiveness is not about letting the other person off the hook. It is about letting ourselves off the hook.

We now understand that all the perpetrator did was offer us a choice of what to believe about ourselves. It was the choices we made that determined how our lives turned out. These choices are the most important part, not the abuse that was inflicted. If the abuse is the thing that determines the path forward, we really would be powerless because we can't go back and change the abuse. It is the belief that drives our perception, and our perception drives our experiences. Therefore, we are not powerless, because we can always change our beliefs.

One last thing about resentment: You have only so much mental capacity and energy during any given day. Every minute you waste in resentment is a minute you could spend building your dreams. Holding resentments makes you powerless in more ways than one. Do not waste any of your energy holding grudges; you are only holding yourself hostage. The other person has probably long since forgotten about whatever abuse they inflicted on you.

The next thing we started to recognize was the level of negativity coming out of other people's mouths. We saw how people with similar levels of negativity would hang out together and gossip about each other. Have you ever noticed that when you're having a conversation with a negative person, no matter what you're talking about, they take that conversation and make it about them? If you're trying to express a feeling or a thought, they have a tendency to take it and turn the conversation around, so it is about their life. They have zero interest in really knowing or understanding you.

As we recognized this in others, we saw some of that in ourselves, which worried us. We matched the words coming out of their mouth to the results of their life and were not impressed by what we saw. As it turns out, most negative people have pretty shitty lives.

We realized the negativity we were verbalizing was costing us and decided we had to stop saying things that made us weak. For James, this meant he had to stop saying just about everything for a while. Sometimes the urge to get back into the victim's negative voice was so strong, he would literally have to bite his lower lip.

Eventually, negative people didn't want to be around us anymore because we no longer supported their narrative. This was okay with us. We were rebuilding our lives and didn't want to poison that process by being surrounded by negativity. When James stopped expressing his victim's voice, his ego was still screaming inside him to tell the story. *Tell the story.* Over time, as he phased out the narrative, the voice kept getting quieter and quieter, until it became silent.

Through watching other people's narratives, we saw that toxic talk created toxic experiences. If you're struggling on the inside, it always starts to reflect on the outside.

Another thing happened that changed and shifted our perspective and started to improve our lives. Many of our friends chose to stand still and not grow or move forward in their own lives, and naturally, we grew apart from them. This result of our life choices further shifted our perspective and continued improving our lives. We often hear teachers and speakers talking about how we need to change the people we are associating with in order to move forward and grow in life. That might seem to force us into a position of breaking up with our friends, but it's not like that.

If you really want to transform your life, know that it is really hard work and really time-consuming to start doing what is necessary. It's going to move you toward new people and experiences. If your current friends do not relate to those people and experiences, you will start drifting apart. It is similar to starting a new romantic relationship, with your friends falling to the side, except in this scenario you are starting a new relationship with yourself and the world around you.

It would be great if all your current friends chose to join you to improve their lives, but the truth is the vast majority of them probably won't. If they are not already there with you, there is probably nothing you can say or do to make them change. We had only one friend who made this journey with us, but even he would check out for years at a time. Then he would return and we would pick right back up where we left off.

Here is the part nobody seems to tell you that was shocking when it started happening to us: Not everyone closest to you right now will stick around for your journey. As you start gaining wealth and influence, some of your friends will hate you for succeeding and some will even blame you for how their lives turned out. It can be ugly.

The reasons vary from person to person, but common feelings are resentment, jealousy, blame, or a sense of entitlement. It is kind of like crabs in a basket. Whenever one almost breaks free, the other crabs pull it back down. We share this with you because, when this starts happening to you, it can be very distracting and heartbreaking. For us, it was always about living with integrity and figuring out if our side of the street was clean.

What does it mean to keep your side of the street clean? It means owning up to your mistakes, apologizing, and doing what you can to make amends. We all make mistakes. Keeping your side of the street clean helps you live without regret. Regret is another waste of energy that can poison and erode your life.

We have this discussion with new people who come into our lives. If they are not committed to personal growth, we probably won't be hanging out with them a year from now. It's not because we don't care for them, it's because we are committed to becoming the best version of ourselves and we will not slow down or stop for anyone.

The same thing can happen in romantic relationships if you want to grow and your partner does not. If you want the relationship to survive, you have to discuss this openly and have clear expectations on what this is going to look like for both of you.

Shifting old beliefs threatens your ego because your ego senses a loss of control. Your ego wants to keep control because control makes you feel safe. In its attempt to gain back control, your ego often goes into attack mode to reinforce the idea that you need its protection. The main tool your ego uses to gain control is projection. Projecting on others means those around you will end up in the crosshairs. It's important for those around you, especially those of significance in your life, to understand perception so they better understand the journey you are on and know what to expect during your time of change. We encourage you to have them read this book if they're willing.

For us, we decided on day one of our relationship that we would always have each other's backs. Depressed or happy, we were in it together. We were committed to working through everything together. Over time, our strengthening relationship restored our faith in humanity.

The last big lesson we had to learn, and are still working on today, was to stop caring about what other people thought of us. We had to eliminate our need to seek validation. After James's childhood experiences, he always felt compelled to prove himself. Let's just say getting out of jail did not reduce that need. When he first got out, he essentially had a huge chip on his shoulder. After a while, he realized that proving himself was distracting him from trying to achieve his goals.

One day, Steph looked at him and said "Just stop! You don't have anything left to prove. Why do you want it so bad?" She was right. He wasn't following his dreams because he was seeking validation instead. When James was able to accept this and let it go, he was able to fully focus on the things he wanted to accomplish. From that point forward, our success began to skyrocket.

Steph also had to quit caring about what people thought of her. She would beat herself up when she failed to exercise or didn't eat perfectly. Our culture says that to be accepted and loved you have to be perfect. Let's face it, women have it much worse than men in this department. We live in a false world of airbrushed models and photo filters. You have to have the perfect body, hair, clothes, and everything else you can imagine in order to fit in. It's exhausting! Especially when we live in a society where we are taught from an early age to compare ourselves with others. All this exacted a steep toll on Steph because she always struggled with her body image after her abuse.

We are going to let you off the hook today. You can finally stop worrying about what other people think of you, because we are going to tell you what they are thinking about. Unless they are jealous of you, they are not thinking about you at all. They are too busy worrying about what you and others think of them. They simply don't care about you. Those who spend all their time gossiping about others only care about themselves. It's time to let it go. There is no bigger waste of time than this.

YOU GOT THIS!

One good thing that came out of all our experiences was that we became extremely adaptable. We have gone through sexual abuse, abandonment, bullying, learning disabilities, emotional abuse, drug addiction, hit men, solitary confinement, a failed suicide attempt, physical abuse, and all sorts of other shit.

Whatever the environment, we adapted. Before James went to jail, he had been jumped by five thugs and beaten into the ground. He had been shot at several times, chased, arrested, had overdosed, and had lost everything he owned more than once. As we started our journey together, we realized there was no situation we couldn't handle. We have been in the worst circumstances imaginable and we're still here. This gave us confidence that we were capable of adapting and handling whatever life might throw at us.

Many people have the fear that a problem will arise that is so big it will overwhelm and break them. When people do break down, it almost always has more to do with the anxiety of what might happen than the reality of what actually does. You have to learn, on a deep level, that you can adapt to just about anything. Knowing you are adaptable is one of the best things to remember when you are struggling. This proved to be an important realization for us as we moved forward.

HOLY SHIT, IT'S WORKING

This is where everything comes together. Through our journey, we realized that if you want to create the things you desire, it comes down to learning how to manage the chaos that exists inside you as it comes out of you. It's worth noting that this is not how you create happiness. We'll cover that later.

You don't know which beliefs your perception is going to draw on to define your current experiences. There is no way to control what is going to come out from moment to moment. Because you have yet to change the source of your assumptions, you have to change what that information means to you in the present. You have to take control of your interpretations, because they drive your direction.

Here is how it works: Your subconscious dishes up a perception of an experience and also gives you an interpretation of what it means to you based on your past experiences. Most people just accept that interpretation as fact and act in accordance with the interpretation. But just because your subconscious drives your perception of any given situation does not mean you have to accept that interpretation as fact. Your conscious mind can reject that interpretation and decide it means something different to you.

Remember, you don't have access to reality. You only have an assumption of what it is and what it means to you. That assumption is based on what this experience meant to you in the past. You have the power to reject that assumption, just as you would if a friend said something really stupid; you wouldn't automatically take it as fact, you would question their assertion and its source.

Question: Have you ever been wrong in the past? The answer for most of us would be, yes, fairly often. Then why would you just take your perception's word for it? When you always believe what you see, you are assuming that your past was perfect.

The real secret of success is learning how to change the meaning of your interpretations. Anyone who has ever accomplished something great in their life knows this is true. Unfortunately, the vast majority of these successful people don't know it consciously, so they attribute their success to something else.

Your perception works like the if/then statement we discussed a few chapters ago. Here is a refresher:

If this happens, then it must mean the same thing to me it meant in the past. If it means the same thing it meant to me in the past, then this is what I should do because it is what I have always done in this type of situation.

All this goes on instantly and automatically with zero input from your conscious mind. Why would your perception assume it means something different this time from what it meant last time? Without a good reason to see it differently, your perception is always going to push you toward what is familiar. If it was safe last time, it should be safe this time.

Most of our lives are lived this way because we assume we see reality. After all, why wouldn't we? It sure feels like reality, even when we learn logically that it isn't. We can't tell the difference, so what difference does the difference make anyway? Well, actually, it makes a huge difference.

We discovered this when, every time we tried to change a belief, something would come up to reinforce the old belief we were trying to move away from. Whenever we worked to change a belief, the opposite always showed up first.

Let's say you have a belief about being dumb and you decide you are going to change that belief to "I am smart." As great as that sounds, your subconscious will continue to reflect the "I am dumb" narrative back to you because you are still seeing through the "I am dumb" filter. The new belief is not yet planted deep in your subconscious mind and, because you are choosing to bring this belief to the forefront of your mind, your perception is now on the lookout for things that reflect the old belief back to you. You will have an increased awareness of experiences that seem to confirm the old belief of feeling dumb.

Stop! Here is your opportunity to change your interpretation. As we've said, you can't instantly insert a new belief deep into your subconscious or stop your mind from using the old belief to make assumptions to define your current situation. This is why the old belief always comes up first. Here is how we turned the tables on our perception and changed the belief. We literally waited for the old belief to come up and, when it did, we used it as our trigger to change our interpretation. When the old beliefs were reflected back to us, we would deny that interpretation and insert the new one in its place. As it relates to the example above, every time we felt dumb we saw this as an opportunity to reaffirm that we were smart.

Your false assumptions give you an opportunity to pull back and say that you no longer believe this. How many times does this happen when you are trying to change a belief? It depends on how strong and deeply imbedded the belief is and the level of conviction you have when you challenge it.

This takes practice. There were countless times in the early days where we got caught up in the emotions of the situation and fell right back into the old belief. This is the trap most of us fall into. We think, "Here is more evidence that I am in fact dumb, so it must be true," not realizing the evidence came from our own mind and is just the old belief being reflected back.

We had a saying, "In your defense lies your truth." Whenever we got emotionally charged or defensive about something, it meant someone had come along and poked at one of our insecurities. We learned to monitor our emotions to see when we got defensive. We would question the reason why and use the information to track our progress toward growth.

It would be great to just wake up and decide to change the beliefs that have held us back our whole life. Unfortunately, we often project and repress our emotions and refuse to fully feel the pain of the situation. There is not enough emotional pain associated with the old belief for our mind to reject the idea immediately and to adopt the new belief. In other words, pain is what sends a signal to our mind telling us it is not an experience we want to repeat. Like it or not, we evolved to learn through pain. The more pain associated with any given experience, the faster we learn.

Here is a simple story to illustrate the point. One day James was cooking in the kitchen. On the hood above our stove are two small lights. James looked up and noticed one of the lights had spots on it from some sauce or something that had splashed up. James reached up with his finger to try and wipe it off. The light was so hot that it severely burned him. When James reached up, he did not believe the light would be hot. Most of the latest bulb technology does not put out that much heat. He was wrong. Those lightbulbs happened to be halogen bulbs, which are extremely hot.

Will James touch that light, or any similar looking light again? Of course not! The amount of pain associated with the experience signaled James's brain to immediately register a new belief about these bulbs. What would have happened if, when he touched the bulb, it was pretty hot but did not burn him? Would that have kept him from touching light bulbs in the future? Probably not! In that scenario, there is not enough pain to cause him to rewrite the underlying belief. But in this case the old belief caused him so much pain, he adopted a new belief to avoid experiencing that pain again. The mind processes emotional pain in much the same way as this example with physical pain.

This is why most people only change when the pain of not changing outweighs the pain of changing. Pain is not our only teacher, but it is a very powerful motivator and the one we default to when we refuse to be an active participant in our own lives. Most people are more motivated by moving away from the things they fear than moving toward the things they want.

Let's look at it from the perspective of the 90 percent of people who fail to change their lifestyle after having coronary bypass surgery. We probably all know someone who failed to change their habits after having a heart attack. Their life was literally on the line, yet they still failed to make the necessary lifestyle changes. Why?

We fail to calculate the cost of not changing, even when it is right in front of us. We live in complete denial. We believe we see the world for what it is because we do not understand the way perception works. This is why it is so important to calculate the cost of doing nothing. In order to stop living in denial, we have to become our greatest adversary. We don't need to beat ourselves up, but we need to learn to challenge ourselves until the idea of doing nothing scares the shit out of us. There is no creativity in conformity and comfort, creativity only exist in chaos and uncertainty. We have to learn to create enough motivation inside of us to drive ourselves into the chaos and uncertainty of change.

Once you have mastered the process of altering your interpretations by breaking free from the chains of conformity, you can start to change your interpretation of everything. We call this empowering your delusion.

Question: What does it mean if we don't have access to reality and all we have is our own interpretation? Does it mean we can always choose to see things however we want? Yes, it does. Does it mean the possibilities are now endless? Yes, they are. If you are catching what we are saying, you just unlocked one of the great secrets of our existence.

You can paint your life whatever color you like. One of the best ways to hack your interpretation is to give everyone and everything the benefit of the doubt. Here is what we mean. Whenever you are left with a choice about how to interpret a situation, always paint it in the best possible light. Why, you ask? To eliminate suffering, of course.

Here is an example: Let's say you walk into a coffee shop and you see a friend sitting in the corner. When your eyes meet, this friend glares at you and gets up and abruptly leaves. What conclusions might you draw from this type of interaction? Like most people, you would probably assume this person is mad at you. Given the situation, this would be a pretty fair assumption. The real question is, would that be the most empowering conclusion you could take away?

If you choose to assume the person is mad at you, you start worrying about why they are upset. How long do you worry? You worry as long as it takes to find out if it is true. The worry could last a day, a week, a year, or even more. How close a friend it is will dictate how much and how long you worry. Either way, whenever that person comes up in a thought or conversation, it will cause a negative reaction.

All this worrying is optional and totally unnecessary. Anytime you are facing a choice about how to look at something, ask yourself one question: Does the way I am choosing to look at this situation serve me? If it doesn't, change it and assume the best.

It does not matter if you choose to interpret things in a positive or negative light. Both positive and negative interpretations are assumptions and are not based in truth.

Because you do not know the truth, why choose an assumption that causes you pain? Either the person is mad at you or they're not. Whichever one it is, leave it until you know for sure. Once you know, you can deal with it then. If you absolutely cannot get it out of your mind, do not wait. Contact the person right away to address the potential issue. Either way, the key is not to stay in suffering any longer than you have to.

People have these terrible assumptions about what other people are thinking and feeling. They leave conversations and situations all the time without seeking clarity. You have to learn to confront this head on and always seek clarity when your assumptions are causing you pain. This is another thing successful people are good at. They are not afraid to have an uncomfortable conversation. This is a must-have trait if you are planning to change your life in any substantive way. You cannot avoid the tough conversations in life.

This concept even applies to complete strangers. One day we were in a store and the clerk was very rude to us. Steph looked at James while we were walking out and said "Wow, that lady hated us."

James looked up and said, "Is that what you took away from that exchange?"

She replied "Yes, what did you take away from it?"

He said, "Anything but that. Maybe her boyfriend dumped her or her dog died." People tend to do this all the time. We choose the least empowering interpretation and, because the situation seems very personal, we assume the worst even when there is nothing at stake. This only hurts us. Most of us have not been taught how emotions work, so we make other people's emotions about us. In reality, their emotions are a reflection of how they feel about themselves.

CHANGE = ELIMINATING CONTRADICTIONS

Stop living in contradiction! Either do the work or change your goal.

After all the work we did on ourselves, we discovered that change came down to one factor: eliminating contradictions. If there is one thing we could say about ourselves, it would be that we became very good at eliminating contradictions. When we found a belief or behavior that was not serving us, we would move to immediately change it.

Just to be clear, we were by no means perfect at this. We failed many times, but we never gave up. Because of this commitment we made to ourselves, we refused to engage in thoughts, behaviors, or habits that we knew were moving us away from the things we wanted in life. This seemed obvious to us, but not to the people around us.

On one occasion, a longtime friend walked into James's office and said, "We have been on this journey a long time together, how come your life continues to get better and mine seems to stand still?"

James replied, "Do you really want to know? Because this could come across as harsh."

"Yes," his friend responded.

"It's easy," said James. "You continually ignore contradictions in your life."

"What do you mean?" replied his friend.

James said, "You constantly come to me for advice and then ignore the suggestions I give you. Even though you know me well enough to know I would never offer you a suggestion not based on research and sound principles, you never follow the advice. Plus, you get really defensive whenever anyone tries to hold you accountable in these areas."

This problem is not unique to our friend in the example above. When you find a solution to an issue in your life and fail to implement it, you start living in contradiction to your best interests. You need to realize you are now causing chaos inside yourself. It is one thing when you are living in ignorance of the problem or solution. It is something totally different when you have discovered the problem, know the answer, and refuse to implement it. You are literally causing yourself to suffer emotionally because you are engaging in behaviors that you know, on some level, are hurting you or those around you.

It is the same thing when you have a goal. Every day you think, "Today is going to be the day I _____ (fill in the blank)." It could be something like working out, eating right, or even getting out of bed at a certain time. When you fail to follow through, you start beating yourself up. This is why we say, "Either do the work, or change your goal." If you're not ready, then you will only cause yourself undue suffering.

This is why it is important to be clear about all the changes you want to accomplish. Prioritize them and then set your goals. Once you have done that, tackle them one change at a time. Set everything else aside. You have to clearly give yourself permission not to do those other things right now. The choice to worry will still come up. You need to have a strong narrative prepared to deal with these choices, because the pattern of wanting these things still exists inside you.

Only when you absolutely know you have the capacity to take on the next thing on your list should you attempt the next change. This is important. If all your goals are randomly floating around in your head, you will be subconsciously beating yourself up about everything you fail to do on a daily basis. All the energy you waste worrying is one of the things preventing you from reaching any of your goals, especially those that are most important. You only have so much time and energy on any given day, so do not waste time beating yourself up for stuff that is not a priority right now.

WAIT, YOU WANT ME TO BE HONEST WITH MYSELF?

If you learn to be honest with yourself, you can identify the patterns dominating your current existence. You can look at how those patterns developed in your past and how they will play out in the future.

Honestly evaluate yourself today. Is your health and fitness getting better or worse? How much do you currently weigh? Is your weight more or less than a year ago? If the current trend continues, how much will you weigh one year from now?

What is the state of your relationships today? Are they deeper and more connected than a year ago, or do you feel like you are regressing? If this trend continues, what will your relationships look like in a year?

How much money or debt do you have? Is your financial situation better or worse than it was last year? If the trend holds, where will you be a year from now?

You can live your life backward as well as forward. What is the status of your career and life pursuits? Have you stalled, or are you more successful and fulfilled? If this trend continues, where will you be this time next year?

There is no mystery here. If you continue to do what you have always done, you will continue to get what you have always gotten, with interest. Something has to change in your patterns if you want different results. If you do not disrupt your current path, you will continue on the same path with similar results. Your ambitions for changing yourself will never happen.

People often seem shocked by the results in their lives. If we take the time to understand cause and effect, the results in our lives often begin to make perfect sense. Take an honest look at your life and the current trajectory in all facets of your life. Look back and you will begin to see how your current results flowed from your thoughts and actions.

It is easy to look at someone else's life and see their trajectories. When you see someone who has spent their entire life eating terribly develop heart disease or diabetes, it's easy to see how their actions contributed to their outcome. When they ask, "Why me?" it's easy for us to look at that person and say, "What did you think was going to happen?"

It is much more difficult to look at our own lives and examine the trends and circumstances shaping our current experience. For us, there was a time when this all seemed very confusing. We couldn't understand why life was so hard. What we did not know is that we were on a path hurtling toward the crashes we experienced. Given the limitations of the beliefs underneath our perceptions, we were more or less destined to get there.

Think about all the different paths in the various aspects of your life. You have a relationship path, a financial path, a health path, a fitness path, and a career path. If you take the time to honestly map the past into the future, you will see where your current path will likely take you. If you let it, this could be the end of denial for you.

When you are thrown into survival mode, all your decisions become fear based. Your life becomes about moving away from the things that scare you rather than moving toward what excites you. It really becomes about needs versus wants. If your underlying survival needs are not met, your wants and dreams are not even an option.

When you adopt a belief system where fear is your reality, then everything you see or do, everything you are, is dictated by the fear that dominates your mind.

If you believe the world is full of hate, all you will see is hate. If you believe the world is out to do you harm, all you will get is harm. Your attempts to steer away from the things you fear will drive you into the arms of what you don't want.

For example, if your greatest fear is of your partner leaving and your relationship ending, you will prepare for what you believe is imminent. You will live with that fear daily and believe it to be true. You will disconnect emotionally and physically from your partner to prepare for the hurt you know you are going to feel when they leave. It is this detachment that causes the other person to become dissatisfied with the relationship and, in the end, it's the reason why they leave.

Here is the real definition of a self-fulfilling prophecy: *When you prepare for a fear you believe is inevitable, you create an environment for that fear to manifest itself in your life.*

CHANGE IS MORE ABOUT STOPPING THAN STARTING

Have you ever stopped and wondered why you do not already have the things you desire most in life? It is because you are taking actions that keep those things away from you. We often hear people talk about this. They often seem to put the blame on something they are failing to do, rather than on something they should stop doing. It's pretty simple, really. Just stop engaging in behaviors that contradict your goals. In doing so, you remove the barriers keeping you from having what you desire.

Simply put, stop asking what you need to start doing to be successful and start asking what you need to stop doing. Success is often more about stopping some behaviors and habits than it is about starting new ones.

Ask yourself this question: "What thoughts, feelings, and behaviors am I currently engaging in that are standing between the person I am now and the person I want to become?"

We focus so much on what we think we need to do that we fail to see the things we need to stop doing. If we want better health, we can focus on the fact that we need to eat healthier, or we can just stop eating the foods that are making us unhealthy. What is the difference? Aren't we just saying the same thing? No. If we don't understand why we make a mistake in the first place, we are doomed to repeat that mistake. In order to foster change we must first eliminate the conditions and contradictions that allow us to be in our current state to begin with.

We have to clear up the problem to make space for the solution. We can't lay a good habit on top of a bad one and expect to succeed. Just like we cannot break off weeds at the surface, leaving the roots, and then plant grass over the top. Eventually, the weeds will push through and take over the grass. This is what Einstein meant when he said, "We can't solve problems by using the same kind of thinking we used when we created them."

You have to solve the problem before you can implement a solution. You likely know people who are at a gym every day working their asses off, but never seem to make any progress when it comes to losing weight. Why? Because the issue is not the fact they were not working out, it is that they are not eating right. They try to implement the solution of working out over the problem of not eating right and they get nowhere.

In order to succeed, they have to solve the underlying problem first. Any good trainer or dietitian will tell you that you can't outrun or outwork a bad diet.

I WILL ALWAYS DRINK SODA

When we first met, James was drinking a lot of soft drinks. Steph would tell him it wasn't good for him and he would say he loved soda and didn't plan to stop drinking it.

Many years later, James began to experience intense brain fog. It was driving Steph crazy. She would say things like, "You never remember anything I say. You are so scatterbrained."

James went to his doctor and had some tests. His doctor told him there was nothing wrong with him and brain fog was just a normal part of aging. We believed there was nothing James could do about it except take some vitamins and hope for the best.

What we discovered later totally shocked us. James went to his doctor for what we thought were unrelated stomach issues. The treatment plan included a strict diet. He couldn't eat any sugar or carbs for several months. He followed the diet as ordered and got very ill for a few days. It seemed weird at the time because it felt similar to how he felt when he came off drugs. After moving through this mysterious illness, he began to feel better and more like his normal self.

When Thanksgiving came, he was ready to take a break from depriving himself of the things he loved to eat. He told Steph he was going to eat whatever he wanted from Thanksgiving to Christmas and would start the treatment again after the holidays. Something really strange happened in the first part of December. His mind was locked in such an intense brain fog that he couldn't think clearly enough to find his car keys. It was then he realized this was how he used to feel every day.

We had totally missed the fact that the brain fog lifted just after he started his strict nutrition treatment. He did not recognize it until the symptoms came back. Not only did his brain fog return, something else he had forgotten about came back as well. His entire body hurt. He felt like he was ninety years old. He had been living with joint pain for a long time before starting treatment.

After doing research, we discovered that sugar causes a lot of inflammation in the mind and in the body. We realized you can't poison your body without poisoning your mind.

This was a very difficult lesson and one James has struggled with often. He has tested it many times, but there is no avoiding it. If he wants to have clarity of mind and a pain-free body, he cannot eat sugar or carbs for more than a few days in a row without paying a price.

We can also honestly say you would not be reading this book right now if James had chosen to live in contradiction and kept eating sugar. Today, James has achieved a level of clarity he previously did not think was possible. After understanding how his system reacts, he knew if he wanted to achieve his goals and accomplish great things, he could never go back to the way he used to eat. This really sucked because he loves the foods he had to give up.

Many of you reading this right now have had similar struggles with sugar. We know people who, on James's advice, gave up sugar for a while. Almost all of them eventually went back to it no matter what the change had done for them. Most of them are also struggling in some areas of their lives because they fail to look at other underlying beliefs driving their self-sabotaging behavior.

This is not an attempt to persuade you to stop eating sugar or anything else. Everyone's body type is unique and reacts differently to various types of food. You just need to understand that everything you eat has an impact on your physical and mental capacity. We can tell you that you are never going to do well if you do not feel well. You might be able to avoid the consequences for a while, but not forever.

You have to find your optimal state of health in order to operate at a higher level. It's all connected. Every choice you make impacts all the other parts of your life. You can't have glaring contradictions in one area of your life without affecting other areas. If you want to move forward in your life, you must stop lying to yourself about the challenges you face.

James spoke at an event recently and a woman came up to him afterward and said, "I loved your speech. I want to bake you a cake and bring it to your office."

James thanked the lady and told her she was very kind. He said, "Please don't bother, I don't want you to waste your time. I don't eat a lot of sugar."

She said, "Oh, what is it with all you self-aware successful people not eating sugar?"

James kind of tilted his head and waited to see if she caught what she had just said. She did and they both laughed. She commented, "Well, maybe there is something to it, but I just can't give up sugar."

Steph found out many years ago that she is sensitive to gluten and dairy. So is one of our children. Even though back then it was hard to find gluten-free and dairy-free food items, Steph made the necessary meal changes to optimize our family's health. It was a challenge, but we did not ignore contradictions. Even when it is super inconvenient, we are committed to doing the work and making the sacrifices necessary to succeed, no matter how many times we fall down on the path. It seems everyone thinks it is the big things that make the difference between success and failure, but they are wrong. It's the thousand little things we choose to ignore that cost us our dreams.

THE THREE CONCEPTS THAT CHANGE EVERYTHING

EVEN A BLIND SQUIRREL CAN FIND A NUT

At some point in your life, you have probably had the thought that success is all about going to college and acquiring some traditional skill set—to become a doctor, lawyer, or technology guru. But what if that thinking is flawed and it is not about skill sets at all, but about information and your ability to acquire and process that information to lead you in the right direction?

Acquiring and processing information is the one thing all the most successful people in the world do better than anyone else. Some people believe this can't be taught or learned. They believe it's something you either have or you don't. That could not be further from the truth.

We are going to share a story to prove, beyond a shadow of a doubt, that right now you have all the skills you need to be successful. All you need to do is gain a fundamental understanding of the concepts shared in this book and implement the three concepts in this chapter, and you will be on your way.

Shortly before we met, James was trying to figure out what direction to take with his life. He went to the local community college and took the entrance exam. When he was done, a woman called him back to give him the results. She told him, in the nicest way possible, he was not going to be able to attend school there. She said, judging by his scores, he would be unable to pass any classes they offered. She suggested he pursue a trade like construction.

Just to be clear, we are not suggesting James is incapable of learning. This is part of the stigma we need to address. Someone not doing well in school is not a reflection of their level of intelligence. Our school systems are set up as a one-size-fits-all solution to learning, which doesn't work for everyone, because one size does not fit all. We all learn differently.

A lot of people fall through the cracks. If that is what happened to you, don't spend one more second feeling like your level of education is any reflection on how smart or capable you are. The sad thing is, the ones left behind by the system are often the truly creative types. The system is set up to teach skills, not foster creativity.

Obviously, the school system failed James in more ways than one. This could have given him all the excuses and justification he needed to stay stuck his whole life. This brings up an important point. The feelings and situations we use to justify our inaction or sense of inadequacy are real. Absolutely, life is unfair, and for some of us, very unfair. It's easy to feel like victims because, in many ways, we are. Here's the question we have to ask ourselves: Does seeing myself as a victim serve me?

In this world, there are no rewards for the people who have lived through the most traumatic circumstances and managed to survive. As a matter of fact, the opposite is true. Most people don't like staring at the dark underbelly of humanity. They don't want to be held accountable for their own stuff, let alone for humanity's problems. Which means that viewing ourselves as victims doesn't serve us on any level. There is no benefit to all the justifications, true or not, we use as reasons for not living up to our potential.

What do you think James did after that day in the college admissions office? Did he go to the city library and start working to learn all the things he had missed in school? If he had, that would have been a great movie. An unprivileged young man, rejected by the system, takes matters into his own hands and graduates top of his class. Great story, but not even close to what happened.

James doubled down on the strengths he already had. James has a great ability to solve problems and, if he believes in something, he can be very persuasive. This is where he started. When he shifted his beliefs in the areas outlined in this chapter, his career took off like a rocket and he never looked back.

James did not have to gain these skills to become successful. Here is the thing about skills: As individuals, we're almost never going to have all the skills necessary to create great things. It almost always takes a team. This means we have to find people to fill in the gaps in our knowledge and skill sets. The most successful people in the world focus on their strengths, understand their weaknesses, and are good at finding great people to fill in those gaps.

Once we finally created the life we desired, we traced back our steps to see what had made the biggest difference. The first thing we found was that it all came down to perception. But which ideas and beliefs did we shift that had the greatest impact on our lives?

We saw that there are just three basic elements that make up our ability to create the life we desire. To be honest, we seemed to luck out when it came to all three. Luck is probably not the right word. We had to change dozens of beliefs to stumble onto the three that seemed to make the biggest difference.

Here is the initial one: When you are forced into survival mode at an early age, your world shrinks as you adopt a very narrow view of yourself and the world around you. You believe, or are made to believe, all the lies you are told about yourself. You take on a very limited view of your capabilities. That, my friend, is the very definition of a fixed mindset.

MINDSET: GROWTH VS. FIXED

As we started to shift and see ourselves, and the world around us, very differently, we started opening up to possibilities. We began to believe we were capable of growing and expanding. We started to adopt a growth mindset and kept building on it with the work we did on ourselves.

Why does having a growth mindset make such a difference in your life? Your perception dictates which opportunities you see and, more importantly, which ones you don't see. You simply cannot grow when you don't recognize the opportunity you have to help move yourself forward in life.

What dictates what you see? It's what you believe is possible. When you have a fixed mindset, you don't believe you are capable of expanding. This severely limits your ability to see any opportunities you might have to grow. No opportunities, no growth! The first idea you need to adopt is that you are capable of growing and expanding. You have to shift your perspective of yourself from negative to positive, and your view of your abilities from fixed to growth.

CAPACITY: SAFE VS. UNSAFE

The second thing we learned is you have to have the capacity to make decisions in order to take on risk and uncertainty. Your mind has been trained to resist taking on more than you can handle at any given time. Why does it determine that threshold? To keep you safe. This is, if you remember, exactly what human perception has evolved to do. At any given point, what signal would you have to send to your perception to indicate you have the capacity to move forward? You must first perceive that you are safe. Only then does your mind and perception have the capacity to decide to take on any new risks.

Your perception of safety dictates your ability to make decisions, as well as your approach to those decisions. This was one of the biggest reasons we both struggled early on. Neither of us felt safe on any level. We couldn't make decisions to move forward because we were stuck in survival mode. We didn't have the capacity, or perception of safety, that would have allowed us to decide to take on enough uncertainty to adopt actual change. Thus, we both stayed stuck for a long time.

The trust we slowly built with one another over time gradually made us feel safer with each other and the world around us. As we began to feel safer inside, our capacity to take on the uncertainty outside us grew as well. This was a big shift for us. We were constantly working to lower each other's walls to allow ourselves to be vulnerable. We have never stopped working with each other, even to this day, and still this ability continues to expand. We make decisions today that we never would have dreamed possible. Here is an important point: As you progress, the feeling of uncertainty never goes away; you just expand your capacity to better handle it.

POWER: RESPONSIBILITY VS. BLAME

The third concept was actually the first one James discovered in his jail cell. You must take responsibility for your life. What does this really do for us? For James, it was a rejection of the idea that he was powerless. In the mind, responsibility equals power.

Would you do something if you knew you would fail, assuming you hadn't promised someone else you would do it? Of course not! Your perception dissuades you from attempting to do things when it believes you will fail.

Blame fills your subconscious mind with doubt about your abilities. When you live in blame, thinking everything is always someone else's fault, essentially you have given away your power. If it is always somebody else's fault, then you don't have the power to change anything because someone else has power over you. Once you establish that you are powerless in a situation, every time you have similar experiences, your perception assumes that you are still powerless.

This perception was very difficult for us to shift. It was tied to all the resentment we felt, associated with all the blame. The amount of power you possess in your life is directly related to the amount of responsibility you take on. If you want more power in your life, find something where you take on more responsibility. Your power, in turn, dictates your ability to take on and sustain positive actions.

Those are the three things you need to change in order to move your life forward: mindset, capacity, and power. These three things connect to opportunity, decisions, and actions. When you approach life with a fixed mindset, feeling unsafe, and looking at your life's results through blame, you may still be able to engage in opportunities, risk, and action. The difference is it will feel like an uphill battle. Everything you do is a fight and is done in resistance instead of flow. We will talk more about resistance vs. flow later. We came to these realizations through extreme amounts of resistance and pain. We are sharing this information in the hope of saving you from some of that pain.

If you perform well in all three areas, your life will take off like a rocket. In the next section we will discuss our assessment that measures these key attributes.

Mindset — Capacity — Power

Welcome to Perception*Sketch*™!

You no longer have to guess how your perception may be negatively impacting the different aspects of your life. We have developed an assessment to help you identify and understand how you perceive the world and the effect these perceptions have on your life.

Below is a brief description of the information included in the assessment, as well as an overview of perception and the three concepts presented in this chapter. Though this section may have some redundancies, we believe this review will help you to fully understand and integrate this information into your lives. For more information, or to take our assessment, go to https://perceptionsketch.com/.

Do you have a growth mindset, the capacity to take opportunity risks, and the power to effect change in your life?

PerceptionSketch is designed to assess the subconscious beliefs that create what your mind perceives as reality. It will help you understand what dictates your decision-making process and how it creates your world. In order for you to fully appreciate the value and meaning of your PerceptionSketch results, you need to first understand that your perception is the one thing that dictates every opportunity you see, every decision you make, and every action you do or do not take.

Why Perception?

To everything you see and experience, you assign meaning using assumptions based on what's happened to you in the past. Your mind is a vast database of memories and experiences categorized into beliefs. Beliefs are essentially decisions you've made to define your world based on your experiences. When you have a new experience, your mind does something similar to a Google search, racing through your memories to find a belief created from similar experiences. It then uses that belief to create an assumption to apply meaning to the current experience.

Your brain processes millions of bits of information a second. You use assumptions because this amount of information is more than the conscious mind can handle. Perception takes all this information and filters it down to what your mind determines are the most critical pieces. Since the time of our earliest ancestors, perception has had one job and one job only, to keep us safe. Perception doesn't care if you are happy or sad, successful or failing, creative or unimaginative, fulfilled or frustrated.

In today's world, while your perception rarely needs to keep you safe from predators, it still helps protect you in some circumstances, such as playing sports or driving a car. Unfortunately, perception doesn't work as well with many of modern life's complexities. Things like problem solving, relationships and taking risks require mindfulness rather than assumptions. It's a shift from survival mode to finding success, and it depends upon how well you:

✓ Recognize opportunities

✓ Decide to embrace risk

✓ Take sustainable action

This is where perception can get in the way, by using assumptions instead of mindfulness to assign meaning to your experiences. While trying to keep you safe, perception can severely limit your ability to recognize opportunities, because to recognize opportunities, your mind has to think creatively instead of making snap decisions. Perception also impacts the way you make decisions. If the beliefs that fuel your assumptions are untrue, then the meaning you put on your experience is inaccurate. When your perception uses fear of the unknown to keep you safe, taking action can be challenging.

As perception uses assumptions to give meaning to your experiences, your life becomes a pattern—your past is casting a shadow over your future. If your life is not what you want it to be, it's not because you have done anything wrong. It's because you made the only decisions you could with the information you had available.

The purpose of Perception*Sketch* is to help you focus on critical perceptions, challenge your assumptions, and, with mindfulness, encourage you to revisit those assumptions and become empowered as you transform your life! It is not a definition of who you are, but rather a snapshot of how your current perceptions might be affecting the way you view your world. Perception*Sketch* will challenge what you consciously believe about yourself. You might not agree 100 percent with the results, but that is by design.

The assessment examines your alignment with twelve specific categories that define the three key attributes of Perception: MINDSET, CAPACITY, and POWER.

We all have a unique blend of natural abilities and an individual mindset. Research shows that people who find lasting fulfillment and success in their lives possess certain key attributes. By managing their perceptions, they rid themselves of false and limiting beliefs that keep them trapped. They empower themselves to face challenges, overcome setbacks, and seize opportunities.

Perception*Sketch* shows you where your perceptions about MINDSET, CAPACITY, and POWER (MCP) are dictating critical aspects of your life. This clarity can help you remove barriers, realize your dreams, and tap into your unlimited potential.

MINDSET

Individuals who perceive their world through a growth mindset instead of a fixed mindset typically embrace challenges and believe in continuous effort. They are more resilient in the face of setbacks and achieve greater and more creative success. Carol Dweck, PhD, the psychologist who coined the terms growth mindset and fixed mindset, maintains that our original natural abilities and qualities can be enhanced. Intelligence is dynamic, personality and character traits evolve, and performance improves.

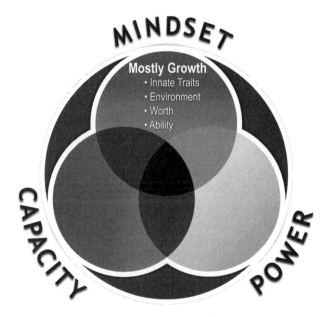

Mindset example: *Your mind takes in millions of pieces of information per second. Perception's job is to quickly reduce all that information down to the bits that are the most important to you, according to your belief system. Essentially, your mind filters out what you don't believe to be probable. When you don't believe something is possible, your mind does not look for, or recognize, opportunities in that area.*

Let's say the thing you want most in life is to find love, but you believe you don't deserve it. That belief gives you a fixed mindset about love, and your perception will blind you to an opportunity in this area, even if someone is flirting with you. A person who believes they deserve love, and that love is possible, has a growth mindset about love. Their perception would be looking for experiences supporting that belief and would be able to see opportunities for love when they happen.

A growth mindset fosters a belief in transformation and empowers you to achieve your full potential. It enables you to see, identify, and overcome the obstacles preventing you from recognizing opportunities you need to pursue. Remember, we can have a fixed mindset in one area of life, and a growth mindset in others.

The MINDSET perception attribute is explained by the four categories below.

1. Innate Traits

Here a growth mindset is a belief that natural talents, abilities, intelligence, personality, and character traits can be enhanced through personal effort, training, and experience. Such transformation will empower us to see and overcome the obstacles that might be preventing us from recognizing the opportunities and challenges that, if pursued, would help us to achieve our full potential. It's not always the people who start out with the most or the best who finish ahead!

2. Environment

If we have a growth mindset in this area we generally believe in the possibility of affecting the conditions, situations, settings, and natural occurrences that surround us. We tend to be continuously managing and improving our environment—dramatically increasing the odds that, when luck shows up, we will be in a position to take advantage of it. Conversely, if we have more of a fixed mindset, we might focus instead on seeking environments where we can depend on what has worked for us in the past. We are less likely to see opportunities to change our world for the better.

3. Worth

This is all about the opinion we have of ourselves and how we perceive our own value. Where do we get our sense of worth? If we have a growth mindset, we find value in the journey more than in the results. We don't let failure get us down because we know failure is an essential step toward success in the journey of life. Our failures actually become the necessary fuel for continued growth, which increases our sense of self-worth. However, if we have a fixed mindset in this area we tend to tie our sense of worth to results instead of absorbing the richness of the journey. Consequently, we seem to direct our energies toward areas where we have found success in the past. Mistakes, criticism, and setbacks can be especially difficult to handle because they impact the perception of our results, which in turn affects our self-worth.

4. Ability

This category is centered on our ability to perform. How do we perceive our adeptness at expressing artistic talent? Showcasing athletic skill? Exhibiting craftsmanship? Demonstrating business acumen? If we have a growth mindset, we shun the idea we will "never be able to do" some particular thing. Instead, we perceive that abilities can be improved, acquired, and cultivated. This belief leads us to confront obstacles and think about what we can do to stretch ourselves. If we have a fixed mindset, we might wonder if we've "already got all we're going to get" as far as natural abilities, which can result in trying to prove ourselves only in areas where we are more skilled.

CAPACITY

Abraham Maslow's often-cited "hierarchy of needs" framework describes the stages of human development. The first is physiological (food, water, warmth and rest), and for most people those needs are met. Next comes safety (physical, emotional, and group acceptance). As those needs are met at the most basic level, we begin to see progress toward self-actualization. Those with sufficient safety will have the capacity to step into uncertainty and take on opportunity risks to maximize their potential.

Capacity example: *Your perception's main job is to keep you safe. What is safe? From perception's point of view, it is whether or not you feel, or believe, you are safe. When you don't feel safe in your life, it is your perception's job to point you in a direction that creates safety for yourself.*

Envision having your dream job presented to you, but it's with a start-up— making it very risky to take. Would you leave a comfortable job you like in order to pursue your dream? If you don't feel safe or secure, you will most likely not have the capacity to take the risk. On the other hand, a person who perceives they are safe and secure in this area will be more likely to take the risk.

When we perceive that our overall safety-based needs have been met, we will have more capacity to decide to step into the uncertainty necessary to achieve our goals. Remember, we can have a lack of capacity in one area of life and still have capacity in another.

The CAPACITY perception attribute is illustrated by the four categories below.

1. Physical Safety

When we have an overall perception of sufficient personal and family safety, it signals a general reconciliation of our feelings from past situations and issues of feeling physically unsafe—abuse, job insecurity, even violence. This means we can feel more comfortable with the idea of taking the necessary risks for pursuing transformational opportunities.

2. Emotional Safety

Are we sometimes emotionally guarded? Are we afraid of someone seeing our true selves? Perhaps we perceive we are emotionally unsafe because of something that happened in our past? We have all been hurt emotionally. Closing ourselves off to relationships and intimacy can be a normal reaction. It is natural to have a fear of being vulnerable, but emotional safety means being comfortable sharing our true self with others when the occasion is right or appropriate. It means letting down our guard, being ourselves right from the start in professional and personal relationships, even speaking our mind in situations where it makes us vulnerable.

3. Group Acceptance

Significant personal power comes from giving less attention to pursuing approval from the "pack." This can liberate us from the need to continually try to prove ourselves, allowing us to concentrate more on things like a good work ethic over seeking than respect. Such perceptions mean we are less likely to pay attention to appearances and what others think of us and more likely to focus on self-actualization.

4. Self-Esteem

Positive self-esteem comes from beliefs created by acting on our talents, staying actively engaged in life, or by attaching ourselves to something apart—a cause, a leader, a group, even the accumulation of wealth. Of these, realizing our talent is the most difficult to accomplish. This doesn't need to be drudgery if we begin by exploring life and enjoying all it has to offer, finding areas of interest for self-development along the way. Even if it takes a catalyst to jump-start the effort, we should remember that most creators in history were prompted, needled, or egged on to greatness. A sufficient level of self-esteem creates a perception of safety within.

POWER

Fundamentally, we either perceive that things just happen to us according to random circumstances and the actions of others, or we believe that we are creators of our experiences. If our perception suggests that nothing is ever our fault, it means that we are giving away our power to affect change.

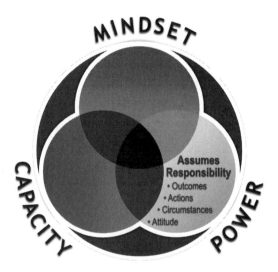

Power example: *Do you perceive that you have power, or do you perceive that you're powerless? Power is about ownership, and ownership is about taking responsibility.*

Imagine the economy is not doing well and this has severely impacted your income. Is the economy to blame for your loss of income, or are you? A person lacking power would believe that the economy is to blame. This perception makes them powerless because they can't control the economy, so they surrender to their fate. They would not be able to take action, because they believe their situation is out of their control. Conversely, a person who has power would take responsibility for their situation, even though it's not entirely their fault.

By taking responsibility, we dictate our own fate by acting to find a way to thrive in any situation. We will never take action unless we believe we have the power and ability to succeed. Learning how to take responsibility for the right things in life (*our own outcomes, actions, circumstances, and attitudes*) vs. the wrong things (*those of other people*) is the difference between becoming a creator and being powerless. Remember, we can lack power in one area of life and have power in another.

The POWER perception attribute is explained by the four categories below.

1. Outcomes

When we take responsibility for our outcomes, instead of blaming luck or others and making excuses, we gain power by owning the results and consequences of every decision, every failure, and every path we choose. When we perceive our outcomes this way, we can learn from our results. This gives us the power to take action to effect change, not only in our lives, but also in the world around us. Whenever we look at negative or unfortunate outcomes as "it's not my fault," we no longer have control and are therefore subject to external forces. We all have within us the power to chart our own course. It's what we choose to believe about ourselves on the basis of what happens to us that determines our fate.

2. Actions

When situations arise, do we act in our best interest, or do we react? Do we perceive our lives to be dictated primarily by the effects of others' actions and by fate? By not taking responsibility for our own actions, we actually surrender our power to those around us, and to our environment. We can all think of times when we acted against our own conscience, or engaged in actions that we knew to be misguided or wrong, and then made excuses for our behavior or blamed others. By taking responsibility for all our actions, we maintain our power to control how we are affected, to create meaningful change, and to capitalize on opportunities for growth.

3. Circumstances

No doubt things can happen that are beyond our individual control, in which someone, some thing, some random occurrence, or just plain luck affects us. When we choose to believe we have no control over negative, unpleasant, and unfortunate situations, it becomes difficult for us to take action and determine our own path. Instead of justifying our behavior by making excuses and placing blame, we can take responsibility and influence those circumstances as much as possible in our favor. This way we create our own luck and shift our circumstances to empower our life, instead of being defined by them.

4. Attitude

Do we take control of our attitudes and respond to events, or simply brace for life's catastrophes? Some of us will interpret challenges in the best possible light, while others will use those challenges as justification for thinking the worst. They will look for excuses and for others to blame. Even in situations that aren't that bad, some will still walk away with only negative feelings. No matter what happens, there's always some percentage of positive and some percentage of negative coming out of every situation. The question is, what do you choose to identify with? By favoring the positive and taking ownership, we foster the ability to accomplish more and acquire real power to reach our full potential!

Aspects of Life

Most of us feel pretty good about some areas of our lives but recognize the need to improve in others. Transformation is possible when we evaluate and change our MINDSET, CAPACITY, and POWER (MCP) perceptions in the following four "playing fields" or *Aspects of Life*. These four areas are key to creating balance, fulfillment, and transformation.

LIFE PURSUITS — *Fulfillment*

This *Aspect of Life* is all about living life to its fullest. It includes such things as our passions, career, education, and life mission. Our perceptions concerning these endeavors and the journey toward our goals is key to feeling like we are living up to our potential. Are we improving our performance abilities? Do we see opportunities for being successful in any environment? Do we take on risky projects to maximize rewards? Do we take personal responsibility for team successes and failures? Is our attitude positive around negative people? Our MCP scores toward our *Life Pursuits* will identify areas of focus for creating a deeper sense of fulfillment.

PHYSICAL WELL-BEING — *Energy*

Weakness in this core *Aspect of Life* makes it more difficult to form deep and meaningful relationships, achieve financial stability, or pursue our goals. In order to maximize our potential, we need abundant energy. Do we follow healthy routines and make time to exercise? Do we attribute our level of health to genetic makeup? What are our perceptions about expanding our physical abilities vs. doing our best with the hand we were dealt? Do we worry about how appearance influences our self-esteem and how people treat us? Do we perceive our self-worth is affected more by effort than by results? Are we feeling safe enough to risk making opportunity decisions to enhance our overall health and fitness? Do we take responsibility for all our actions and outcomes? Our MCP scores will show us areas of focus to help improve our *Physical Well-Being.*

FINANCES — *Security & Resources*

While this *Aspect of Life* is essential for sustaining basic needs for food, shelter, and safety, it is also critical for fueling our pursuits, health and fitness, and relationships. Do we perceive acquiring wealth is influenced more by our circumstances than by our ability to see different possibilities? Does the idea of risking and losing money make us anxious? Do we believe that it's our choices, or our job, the economy, and other factors that determine our financial situation? Our MCP alignment shows the areas of focus to help us improve in the area of Finances.

RELATIONSHIPS — *Love & Joy*

Even with the fulfillment, energy, and security from the other *Aspects of Life*, our lives would be empty without the love and joy that we can feel in relationships—and it's our perceptions that dictate the health of those relationships. Do we surround ourselves with friends who have our back no matter what, or do we prefer friends that push, test, and challenge us? To what degree do we value candidness? Do we present ourselves as "I am who I am and what you see is what you get"? Or do we believe that we can create chemistry with anyone? Is it our view that nothing can change in our relationships until we do, by taking responsibility instead of blaming and making excuses? Do we feel safe enough within them to be an open book? Vulnerability is the key to developing deeper relationships. Our MCP scores help to identify potential blind spots and areas of focus for helping us enhance our *Relationships*.

THE 8 PERCEPTION*SKETCH*™ TYPES

The pattern of your responses to the assessment's forty-eight questions determines your alignment with the three key perception attributes: MINDSET, CAPACITY, and POWER. The results indicate which of the eight zones is your perception profile, or *Sketch*, and outlines your relevant strengths, abilities, attitudes, and mindset regarding your current approach to life. Each *Sketch* type creates its world in a different way.

Here are descriptions of all the Perception*Sketch* types so you can better understand family members, colleagues, partners, team members, supporters, and other stakeholders who might have any particular one of the eight *Sketch* types.

The key difference between Perception*Sketch* and the more commonly recognized personality type profiles is that Perception*Sketch* is a snapshot of how you approach life. You may also find these brief summaries useful if you have an interest in working to become aligned with one of the other *Sketch* types.

CREATOR

Sees opportunity, decides to embrace risk, and takes sustainable action.

Individuals operating in the Creator zone fundamentally believe they are the architects of their own experiences. They are typically motivated by the need to learn and grow through curiosity and an objective view of life. They tend to embrace fear and anxious feelings as growth opportunities, and quickly remove contradictions from their lives. Creators epitomize two famous quotes: "No problem can be solved by the same kind of thinking that created it" (Albert Einstein) and "Opportunity is missed by most people because it is dressed in overalls and looks like work" (Thomas Edison).

Some Creators have come from the depths of human suffering. Others have been in a static frame of mind, but then made the choice to start living life on new terms. By choosing a growth MINDSET to challenge their perceptions for creating new and empowered beliefs, leveraging their CAPACITY to take on opportunity risk, and exercising POWER through sustainable action, they continue to create the life they desire. Creators learn to be comfortable with being uncomfortable, but are not without their own challenges. They can become contented or satisfied with where they are, and risk stagnation or perhaps decline. They are Creators because of their willingness to accept they might be wrong and their belief that life still has many lessons in store for them.

Creators will benefit from periodic reflections on what brought them to where they are: a growth MINDSET for seeing opportunities, a sense of sufficient CAPACITY that allows them to feel comfortable making decisions to take appropriate risks, and POWER to own every aspect of their lives.

CATALYST

Sees opportunity and considers the risks, while others see limitation.

Catalysts have a strong ability to ignite change. They approach life with an open mind and visionary ideas, being fully prepared to take the risk of going for it. This is all because they tend to have a growth MINDSET, which reflects a belief that personal traits and performance abilities can evolve, and that success is possible in any environment. They likely have sufficient CAPACITY as well, essentially feeling safe enough to make risk decisions for maximizing growth opportunities, even if failure would make them look bad. Catalysts seem to embrace both success and failure as part of life and move on.

However, Catalysts may struggle when it comes to actually pursuing those goals. What keeps them in the starting blocks might be a tendency to blame external influences, the actions of others, and random circumstances for what happens in their life. They might use trials and unpleasant events as justification for thinking the worst when someone, some thing, or just plain luck affects them. Catalysts essentially lose their POWER to chart their own course by not taking ownership for the right things in life (*our own outcomes, actions, circumstances, and attitudes*) vs. the wrong things (*those of other people*).

Catalysts can increase their POWER to take sustainable action when they assume responsibility for all aspects of life, such as: failed projects, their perspective on their relationships, bad financial investments, a negative work environment, or poor health and fitness. This transformation is only possible when they identify and challenge any experiences or beliefs that cause them to surrender their POWER.

GRITTY

Loves a challenge, pursues growth,
and controls their life by taking responsibility.

Those in the Gritty zone tackle life's challenges by maintaining a growth MINDSET and acting with POWER despite perceptions of having limited CAPACITY to take on the opportunity risks necessary to maximize their full potential.

What keeps them going is their ability to face life's obstacles with a belief that transformation is possible through sustained activity, and often by outworking those around them. Fueled by the hope of improving their situation, they endure, adapt, and overcome in pursuit of their goals. Much of their grittiness comes from the POWER they gain from taking responsibility for their actions and attitudes instead of making excuses and blaming random circumstances or the actions of others for what happens in life.

The Gritty person's struggle with taking on risk stems from feelings of insufficient safety and security. This can occur when they: feel threatened by current or past situations, worry about appearances and what others think, might struggle financially, and are uncomfortable sharing their true self with others. Consequently, they have a tendency to continually try proving themselves and may feel forced into coping actions not of their choosing, instead of directing their MINDSET and POWER toward growth and personal evolution.

Gritty individuals can increase their CAPACITY to step into uncertainty once they perceive security in areas such as: their physical needs, being vulnerable when appropriate, their own identity in their relationships with others, or embracing their successes and failures as a part of life. This transformation is only possible when they identify and challenge any beliefs and experiences that are creating the perception of a lack of safety and inhibiting their CAPACITY to take opportunity risks.

GUARDIAN

Faces uncertainty head on and has the power to tackle obstacles.

Guardians operate from a perception of relative security, which gives them the CAPACITY to decide to take on opportunity risks. They generally meet life's challenges by owning their actions and attitudes, instead of making excuses and blaming random circumstances or the actions of others for what happens in life. Guardians have POWER by taking responsibility for failures, correcting errors, and responding to challenges instead of bracing for life's catastrophes. They tend to interpret situations in the best possible light when someone, some thing, or just plain luck affects them.

Guardians, however, tend to view the world with a somewhat fixed MINDSET, which leads them to a status quo approach to life. They may be a little set in their ways and not as open to exploring transformational opportunities. Guardians may also view challenges as something to be fixed or corrected, rather than embracing them as learning experiences. They typically try to prove themselves in comfortable areas where they are more skilled. Even though they might easily excel, they are also reluctant to take on more-difficult projects because they would consider any failure damaging to their self-worth.

Guardians can move from a fixed to a growth MINDSET once they believe: that they are able to influence their environment, that making progress toward goals creates a sense of worth, that they can be successful in any environment, or that their natural talents can evolve. This transformation is only possible when they identify and challenge any experiences that created the beliefs driving their perception of a fixed MINDSET.

OPTIMIST

**Sees the potential for growth
and is resilient in the face of setbacks.**

Those in the Optimist zone are defined by their growth MINDSET. Their belief that personal traits and performance abilities can evolve allows them to see more opportunities for growth! They typically love a challenge and will generally tolerate mistakes, criticism, or setbacks. While most Optimists are confident in their ability to learn and improve, they should remember that an idea that is realized is always more valuable than an idea that's still in their head.

What slows down Optimists in their transformational journey is a perception of limited CAPACITY to take on opportunity risks to maximize their potential. This might stem from feelings of insufficient safety and security such as: feeling threatened by current or past situations, worrying about appearances, struggling financially, and discomfort sharing their true self with others. Consequently, Optimists tend toward trying to prove themselves, instead of pursuing personal evolution.

Also holding back the Optimist could be a tendency to avoid taking ownership of life's unfortunate situations. They likely perceive that things "just happen" to them because of random circumstances and the actions of others. They might often make excuses and blame external factors for their actions and attitudes. Optimists essentially lose their POWER to chart their own course by not taking ownership for the right things in life (*our own outcomes, actions, circumstances, and attitudes*) vs. the wrong things (*those of other people*).

Optimists can increase their CAPACITY to step into uncertainty once they perceive security in areas such as: their physical needs, being vulnerable when appropriate, their own identity in relationships, or embracing their successes and failures as a part of life. They will regain their POWER to take sustainable action in all aspects of life when they assume responsibility for things such as: failed projects, their perspective toward their relationships, bad financial investments, a negative work environment, or poor health and fitness. Their transformation is only possible when they identify and challenge any beliefs and experiences that are creating perceptions of insufficient CAPACITY and the surrender of their POWER.

SENTINEL

Is genuine and vulnerable
by being grounded in the self.

While those in the Sentinel zone may not be fully engaged in life's growth journey, they are poised to get off the sidelines and begin their transformation! They have the CAPACITY to make opportunity decisions—feeling safe enough to take on risks to pursue their true potential. This capability comes from perceptions of physical and emotional safety, a comfortable connection to their pack, and sufficient self-esteem.

Sentinels tend to hesitate, however, to engage and move forward. This reluctance is partly tied to a fixed MINDSET, possibly caused by perceptions that their innate abilities and qualities generally won't evolve, and that performance is unlikely to improve. Rather than trying and failing, Sentinels tend to avoid opportunities where success is not likely, since failure would lessen their sense of self-worth. This fixed mindset can blind SENTINELs to avenues for growth.

Also holding them back could be a tendency to blame external influences, the actions of others, and random circumstances for what happens in life. When adversity affects them, Sentinels may lose their POWER to dictate their future by not taking ownership of the right things in life (*our own outcomes, actions, circumstances, and attitudes*) vs. the wrong things (*those of other people*).

Sentinels can move from a fixed to a growth MINDSET once they believe: they are able to influence their circumstances, that making progress toward goals creates a sense of worth, that they can be successful in any environment, or that their natural talents can evolve. They will also regain their POWER to take sustainable action in the various aspects of life when they assume responsibility for things such as: failed projects, their perspective on their relationships, bad financial investments, a negative work environment, or poor health and fitness. This transformation is only possible when they identify and challenge any experiences and beliefs that drive their perception of a fixed MINDSET, and cause them to surrender their POWER.

SURVIVOR

Shoulders responsibility, blows through obstacles,
and doesn't make excuses.

The goal for Survivors is to "just keep swimming and keep your head above water." They meet life's trials by owning their actions and attitudes, instead of making excuses or blaming others for what happens in life. They take responsibility for failures and respond to challenges, instead of simply bracing for life's catastrophes. Survivors have the POWER to achieve faster and more sustainable results by taking ownership of the right things in life (*our own outcomes, actions, circumstances, and attitudes*) vs. the wrong things (*those of other people*).

But instead of seeing opportunities for growth, Survivors seem to be stuck in a rut because of a mostly fixed MINDSET—perceptions that their innate abilities won't evolve, and that performance is unlikely to improve. Rather than trying and failing, Survivors tend to avoid opportunities where success is unlikely, which would lessen their sense of self-worth.

Survivors also perceive a limited CAPACITY to take on the risk of pursuing the very opportunities that could help them realize their true potential.

This stems from feeling insufficiently safe because of current or past situations, worrying about appearances, struggling financially, and discomfort about being vulnerable. Consequently, they may try to prove themselves instead of directing their POWER toward growth and personal evolution.

Survivors can move from a fixed to a growth MINDSET once they believe: they are able to influence their circumstances, that making progress toward their goals creates a sense of worth, that they can be successful in any environment, or that their natural talents can evolve. They can increase their CAPACITY to step into uncertainty once they perceive security in areas such as: their physical needs, being vulnerable when appropriate, their own identity in relationships, or in embracing their successes and failures. This transformation is only possible when they identify and challenge any experiences and beliefs driving their perception of a fixed MINDSET, and their limited CAPACITY to take opportunity risks.

STATIC

Resists change either by choice,
or held back by their perception.

There are two types of individuals in the Static zone—those who are complacent in life by choice, and those who are held static by their perceptions. You can tell which one you are by asking yourself: "Am I content with my life as it is now, or do I desire change in the various aspects of my life?"

Whether you are here by choice, or are held Static by your perceptions, your approach to life is in heavy resistance. If you are here by choice you may be resisting change in order to preserve your status quo. For those held Static by their perception, it may feel like no matter how hard you fight you seem to get either the same or worse results. Everyone has found themselves in this state at some point in their life. But for those willing to understand themselves better and explore how perception works, this is the beginning of creating the life they desire.

The first step is to address their fixed MINDSET, which makes it difficult to see opportunities for achieving their goals. Next is expanding their limited CAPACITY to step into uncertainty and take the risks necessary to get what they want. The final struggle can be finding the motivation to take sustainable action. This occurs when they give their POWER away by blaming or assigning responsibility to anything or anyone other than themselves.

Static types can adopt a growth MINDSET once they believe: they can influence their circumstances, that making progress toward their goals creates a sense of worth, that they can be successful in any environment, or that their natural qualities can evolve. They can also increase their CAPACITY to take risks once they perceive security in areas such as: their physical needs, being vulnerable when appropriate, their own identity in relationships, or embracing their successes and failures as a part of life.

And Static individuals will regain their POWER to take sustainable action in various aspects of life when they assume responsibility for things such as: failed projects, their perspective on their relationships, bad financial investments, a negative work environment, or poor health and fitness.

This transformation will be possible when they identify and challenge any beliefs and experiences that are driving their perception of a fixed MINDSET, an insufficient CAPACITY to take opportunity risks, and the surrender of their POWER.

FALSE DREAM SEEMED REAL

MONEY, MONEY, MONEY . . . MONEY

If somebody were to tell you that money doesn't buy happiness, you would probably nod and agree. But deep down inside, you actually wouldn't believe it, would you? We certainly didn't. No matter how many times we heard it, we rejected the idea. We believed it was just something rich people said to make poor people feel better about being poor.

Did you know that the suicide rate is much higher among wealthy people?

If this surprises you, then you're not alone. Most people are shocked by this statistic. Why is the suicide rate higher among rich people? We believe it's because those with money no longer live under the illusion that money is going to make them happy. When you work your whole life to achieve something, it is a huge disappointment to discover that the emotion you attached to that accomplishment does not materialize. Remember, the only reason you do anything is to feel the emotion you believe will be associated with that experience. If you believe money buys happiness, you are going to be crushed when you find out it doesn't.

It wasn't until we made our first million that we realized this was true. We were actually pretty disappointed. We kept pushing up the amount of money we thought it took to be happy. One day we looked at each other and both acknowledged that, even though we had everything we had ever wanted out of life, we had not found happiness. At that point we began a new quest to discover what it truly takes to be happy.

IT'S TRUE, DAMN IT. WHAT NOW?

We eventually learned that what is required to make money is not the same as what must be done to foster happiness. One thing the two have in common, however, is that they are both based on perception. Making money and acquiring possessions is all about managing our perceptions of the outside world. Fostering happiness has everything to do with shifting our perceptions within our inside world.

Hacking our perception to consciously create the things we want is accomplished by managing our perception post-assumption (changing the meaning of the information after it comes out). Happiness is about shifting the emotion and interpretation of past events in our subconscious mind (changing the information before it comes out).

It is often said that the only choice we have is between love and fear. This is true. Unfortunately, it is actually possible to create what we desire in the outside world from a place of fear. As a matter of fact, almost everything you see in the world was created out of a fear for survival.

True happiness, well-being, and connection can only be fostered in love. If we want to find our authentic selves, we have to dig through the layers of fear that exist inside of us and question the lies that monopolize the center of our being.

Most people choose one of the two paths—chasing either internal happiness or external creation—by naively believing that one leads to the other. They don't lead to each other! This means most people end up in one of three categories: those who succeed at creating material wealth but are unhappy; Those who attain happiness but are broke; and those who failed to achieve either wealth or happiness and die poor and miserable.

But there is also a fourth category . . . the magical few who seem to have it all.

INTERNAL HAPPINESS

	MISERY	JOY
WEALTH	Wealthy but Miserable	Wealthy and Happy
SCARCITY	Poor and Miserable	Happy but Broke

EXTERNAL CREATION

We want you to have the information you need to join those who have both wealth and happiness!

We discovered that we can reshape both our internal and external worlds at the same time. This is actually the easiest and most productive way to do it. The problem is that most teachers, preachers, coaches, therapists, motivators, and gurus typically focus on one or the other because that is what they know. The good news is, we will teach you how to create and shape your perception on the inside and on the outside. This is the only way to become a complete human being.

There are self-help books on how to create material success and there are other books on how to feel happy and fulfilled. These two ideas are generally treated as mutually exclusive. This book brings them together.

We have already covered how to hack your perception about the outside world. In the next few chapters, we will teach you the Emotional Integration Technique. This process is about shifting your internal experience. It is possible to conquer the inside world in such a way that it has a profound effect on the outside world. The inside always affects the outside.

In today's world, most people are concerned more with the outside than the inside. They focus on shifting their outside circumstances before even considering what it takes to shift on the inside. This is because the outside is where they pin their misery and fear. They don't understand that the two are the same. Their pain exists on the inside, yet they go outside to try to fix it. If they don't go inside first, the best they can hope for is managing the suffering. What they feel on the inside always reflects on the outside. There shouldn't have to be a choice between the two.

The fastest and most productive way to reshape your world is to approach problems from the inside out. But if you're still convinced on some level that the material world will fulfill you, then we encourage you to pursue that first. Everything you need to know to create wealth and success in your life is in the previous chapters. Just know that it is going to be a long and bumpy ride.

We are, in our inherent natures, creators who also need to feel connected to the people around us. We need both to be whole.

PART FIVE

EMERGING FROM FOG:

THE REAL JOURNEY BEGINS

IDENTIFY AND ERADICATE YOUR FEARS

MANAGING YOUR SHADOW

As Steph and I wrapped up the material-success piece of our lives, we realized there had to be more to self-discovery. We felt like there were still some important things we were missing. We had the material success we had always dreamed of, but our insecurities, while less visible, were still present.

The way we approached our financial success was very logical. We had attempted to shift emotionally along the way. We did a lot of meditations and affirmations and even some mainstream forms of therapy. We learned to manage the darkness, but by no means had it disappeared. We still felt empty.

We became master managers of the parts of us that didn't facilitate what we believed to be in our best interest. We figured out how to manage them better than most people, but the sources of our anger, sadness, and resentment still haunted our existence.

MEDITATION REIMAGINED

We both have been meditating for years. Steph is a more visual person than James, and her meditations always went much deeper. We were taught that meditation is based on clearing the mind. We found this to be extremely difficult because our minds were constantly active. Even though we didn't feel like we were getting the results we wanted, we were both very dedicated to it. Occasionally we would have a very deep meditation that would provide a glimmer of hope, but most of the time we just sat there trying to clear our crazy minds.

Honestly, sometimes our meditations felt like a waste of time. If we had to choose between working out and meditation, meditation always took a backseat. As we started figuring out how to create happiness, we doubled down on our meditations. We were constantly meditating on the beliefs we were trying to shift. It would seem like we were making progress, but then a trigger would hit and reveal that the old belief was still in place.

This was a very frustrating time in our lives, because the more we talked about these beliefs, the more it was like stirring up the bottom of a pond until the water became dirty. As we continued, all sorts of emotions would come to the surface. We couldn't seem to get rid of them, and it caused great chaos in our lives.

Then one day we went to dinner with a friend. He had also invited a guy named Andrew to join us. James asked Andrew what he did for a living and Andrew smiled and said, "Well, it's a little hard to explain. I help people process emotions." James was excited to hear this because that was the very place where we were stuck. He asked Andrew to explain how it worked.

Andrew smiled again and paused before saying, "Here's the thing. I used to be a standup comedian and would spend my days surfing and my nights at the comedy clubs. One day several years ago I got hit in the back of the head with a surfboard. While I was healing, something unusual happened. It took a lot of work to get through the pain I was experiencing, but, once I pushed through, I was somehow able to feel other people's emotions."

James, being a skeptic, looked across the table and asked, "Can you feel my emotions?"

Andrew declined, saying he would never feel somebody's emotions without their permission. James looked at Andrew and said, "Feel away."

"I'm happy to do that, but there's something you need to know first," Andrew replied. He explained that emotions, especially emotions caused by traumatic experiences, get stored in the body, not just in the mind. When asked what that meant, Andrew guided James through an exercise.

Andrew asked James to bring up different emotions tied to various events in his life, then to feel those emotions as best he could. James began the process, and after a few moments, Andrew began mentioning different parts of the body and listing some of the emotions that were stored in those areas. James immediately realized he could feel the anger in his chest and stomach. Andrew explained that this is where James stores anger in his body.

For the next two hours, Andrew took James on a tour of the emotional traumas stored in James's body. The rest of us watched awkwardly as we continued to eat. After they were done, Andrew told everyone how our emotions stay stuck in our nervous system until we process them. He then gave us some suggestions on how we might approach releasing those emotional blocks. He concluded by telling us we needed to honor and express gratitude for all our past fears in order to release them.

This conversation intrigued James. The next morning he woke up early and began to meditate. We had both considered meditation to be about expansion of the mind and had never really considered its impact on the body. With our new knowledge, James focused his meditation on going into his body rather than his mind. He started looking for discomfort and, as he found it, he tried to determine if each kind of discomfort was in some way tied to an emotion.

The first discomfort he focused on was in his shoulders. They felt heavy and tense. He sat and concentrated on that tension. As he focused on that tension, he tried to understand if there was an emotional source for what he was feeling. It didn't take long for him to realize that, because of the life path he had taken, he felt the weight of the world on his shoulders, and this was connected to his feeling overwhelmed so often. It's worth noting that this exercise took James to a deeper meditative state than he had ever accomplished in his life to that point.

As he shifted his focus from the tension to the pain, he realized the feeling in his shoulders was tied to a fear of not being good enough. He zeroed in on determining the role of this fear and this pain. He began to question where and why he had adopted it in the first place and how the fear and pain served him.

He came to realize he had embraced this belief because he had doubted his ability to survive or to succeed in the world. This belief of not being good enough proved to be untrue because he did survive and he had succeeded. The shoulder pain and weight he was now feeling is what motivated him to go forward, even when he didn't want to.

He realized this fear had once served a purpose in his life, but it was now holding him back. With this new realization, he focused on changing the belief to "I am enough." He became grateful for the weight he felt in his shoulders. He understood he had needed a big push at that time in his life and had adopted the fear and used it as fuel. He honored and thanked that fear for the great service it had provided him. He acknowledged this fear had served him at one point but was no longer needed. He focused on the pain and released it.

James continued through his body, identifying discomfort. He worked to eliminate the source or fear that had created each one. After this meditation was over, he felt tremendous relief. He felt as if a million pounds had been lifted off his shoulders. The final thing he noticed was that his mind was so clear he could hear what he could only describe as "white noise."

Over time, we both realized that the mistake we had been making in meditation was trying to eliminate the noise in our head instead of understanding that the noise was coming from disturbances we were feeling in our bodies. Those disturbances were actually fears, which were the source of our worry and anxiety. Essentially they were the dialogue, the noise, that was constantly going through our heads.

Together we started experimenting with different techniques. One day we went into meditation and did not feel any immediate discomfort in our bodies, so we started bringing up various beliefs and feeling their gravity. Then we brought up the associated emotions, found where they showed up in our bodies, and then released them. At the end of each meditation, we felt even more relief.

On one occasion, we went in and started going through our lives in chronological order, reliving in our minds all the traumatic experiences we felt. We found where each experience showed up in our bodies and released those pain points one by one. At the conclusion of that process, we both felt like brand-new people.

We began to feel a sense of peace and happiness at the end of each meditation. After alleviating all the disruptions, the distracting internal noise went away. We could feel our breath moving deeper into our bodies, deeper than ever before. We could feel the energy pulse through us freely with no resistance and hear the very calming sound of the white noise. We realized the white noise had always been there, it had just been obscured by all the distracting internal noise. The best way to describe this place is that it felt like home, like the space we needed to get to and touch every single day. We looked forward to waking up early every morning to find this space together.

Learning to navigate through our bodies entirely changed the power of meditation for us. We realized that the source of the noise in our heads was the emotions trapped in our bodies. The key was to find the pent-up emotions and mini-traumas and process them, not ignore them. Anyone can learn to be mindful of what their body is trying to tell them and, in doing so, find greater depths of inner peace and self-understanding.

OH YES, THERE IS SCIENCE BEHIND THIS TOO . . .

Here is a question for you.

What is the purpose of fear?

The answer is quite straightforward: to keep us safe!

While fear has a negative connotation, it does serve as our protector. Once you set up a fear as a guard, it will stay in place until you release it. These guards become patterns that bring up emotions stored in the body, and they can eventually start to cause havoc in your body. Your childhood fears likely don't serve you as an adult. You no longer need fears that don't serve you, but they don't disappear on their own. They stay in place doing their unrelenting job of trying to protect you.

Those trapped fears and emotions interfere with your body's energy. Each traumatic experience is a bundle of energy that has taken up residence somewhere in your nervous system. If your trauma or stress experience remains unprocessed, its energy will remain dormant in your body until a similar experience in your life retriggers it.

For better mental and physical health, trapped energy needs to be released. An entire field of psychology called somatics (somatic means "affecting the body") tackles this problem with practical applications. One pioneer in the field, Peter A. Levine, PhD, is an expert in medical biophysics. Dr. Levine has spent five decades studying and treating stress and trauma. He originated Somatic Experiencing as a body awareness technique to access fears, stressors, and traumas accumulated in the body. The process enables a person to release and heal these wounds using movement or bodywork (massage).

None of this should be dismissed as fringe, woo-woo stuff. Search through the scientific literature and you will find peer-reviewed studies of effective somatic approaches to fostering emotional resiliency. These twenty-first century studies have appeared in such science journals as *Frontiers of Human Neuroscience* and *Frontiers of Psychology.*

Also at the forefront of Somatic Experiencing was Candace Pert, PhD, a neuroscientist at the National Institutes of Health. Dr. Pert wrote a book entitled, *Molecules of Emotion,* in which she made the case that our bodies are our subconscious mind and our physical bodies can be changed by the emotions we experience. In the book she describes how emotional memory is stored in many places in the body, not just, or even primarily, in the brain. The real true emotions that need to be expressed are in the body, trying to move up and be expressed and thereby integrated, made whole, and healed. In being expressed, emotions can be released—even old emotions stored in body memory.

As always, when this process started working for us, we wanted to know why. We were thrilled to find an abundance of scientific studies to support somatic or body meditation. Many people teach it and believe that this was the meditation practice the Buddha taught when he was alive.

How does this process relate to our understanding of perception? We once saw a movie where a scientist said, "There is no time in mind," meaning that our mind cannot tell the difference between having an experience the first time and a memory. This idea has always intrigued us. We wondered, What if you could have a redo on some of your past traumatic experiences and come out with a different result? We tried this many times with the traditional forms of meditation without finding success.

Once we started meditating with our focus on the body, things started to move quickly for us. We learned to "take out the emotional trash" from our accumulated negative life experiences in order to move through the trauma we had experienced in the past.

In the next chapter we will show you how to use this method to honor and eliminate the false and limiting beliefs connected to your fears. Most importantly, we will help you understand how to release them. You will learn where your fears live and how to root them out.

Somatic meditation is about going within yourself to perform a clearing process. It's about identifying emotional blockages and processing the emotions you repressed in the past. Once you understand how your fears are stored in your body and gain the ability to discover the source of discomfort, you can go in and activate those fears and process them.

CHAPTER

16

THE EMOTIONAL INTEGRATION TECHNIQUE

FOUR WAYS TO IDENTIFY YOUR FEARS

We constantly demonize fear in our culture, even though its only purpose is to keep us safe. It is important here to revisit and gain a deeper understanding of the purpose fear plays in our lives.

When we were children, we did not have the mental or physical capacity to defend ourselves. Fear filled that role and served the purpose of protecting us. Fear drives us to run away. Fear puts up emotional walls to prevent us from feeling the pain of abuse and to prevent access to our hearts to protect them from getting broken. Fear can even move us to develop a new persona, or idea of ourselves, we believe will be accepted when our authentic part has been rejected.

Here is the question you need to ask yourself: "Do my childhood fears still make sense now that I am an adult?" In most cases, the answer is no. What once served you no longer does, but that fear stays in place, like a security guard frozen at attention, until you release it. You can't truly release fear by demonizing and alienating it. You must accept it, honor it, and even love it for the valid purpose it once served in your life.

Again, the key to the Emotional Integration Technique is to go into your body and discover the source of your fear and where it lives. You need to understand and realize the fear was born out of necessity and was put in place to protect you. Look back through your life at different circumstances that took place and imagine your young self putting up one of those security guards to protect you every time something bad or traumatic happened to you. You unconsciously told that guard to protect you every time something like this happens again. Over time, those fear guards only got better and stronger.

There are many of those guards still on duty playing different roles for different types of situations. You have long since forgotten where many of them are stationed. Your job is to go in and find the guards that should have been phased out years ago. Honor them for their service, release them from their obligations, and relieve them from duty.

Here are four different ways to find and identify fears and traumas that are trapped in your body.

The first one is to start with the physical pain. Go into a meditation and find the pain and discomfort that exists in your body. Feel into it and try to let the pain tell you its source. All the pain in your body has a memory attached to it. As you are feeling that pain, let your mind move to the first time you remember feeling that same pain. Once you find it, take the time to understand its source and the fear tied to the discomfort. You can't attempt to release the fear until you find it and understand the reason for it.

The second way is to bring up a false belief or fear you already know you have. For example, "I'm not good enough," "I'm not smart enough," "I'm not lovable enough." Or the fear of failure, fear of intimacy, fear of abandonment. It can be helpful to make a list of every one of the fears you can identify.

Bring up the fear or belief and allow yourself to feel it. Track it back to where it lives inside your body and to the experience that generated this belief. Understand why you adopted it in the first place and realize that it was once useful. Then ask yourself if this belief still serves you. Your mind will not let you release a belief that it believes still serves you in some capacity.

The third way is to go into your life, starting at the beginning of your childhood. Go through the traumatic events you experienced, one by one, and bring up the feelings and beliefs you adopted as part of living through it. Allow this to fill you up until you feel discomfort in your entire body. Then use the Emotional Integration Technique to move through and release it point by point, or body part by body part—one experience at a time.

This is an intense top-to-bottom cleansing. When you complete the third technique you should feel a tremendous release and relief. Even though you will feel a greater sense of peace, all the guards are not yet gone. Basically, you have scraped off a surface layer to give yourself a clean slate on which to work.

Maintenance mode is the fourth and final step. Here is an analogy: The third technique we just discussed is like washing a stack of dishes in the sink. We know there will always be more dishes to clean, so we move forward in maintenance mode, washing one dish at a time to start clearing away the pile. It's the same with this step of the Emotional Integration Technique. It's a daily exercise to start stripping away one or two beliefs at a time.

Everyone has emotional triggers. Living life will bring out buried fears that you might not have caught in the previous techniques. People and situations will trigger negative emotions. Negative emotions are key to isolating all the fears inside us. We can find negative emotions through learning to understand the real purpose that emotions play in our lives. Our emotions were never meant to be a source of drama. They are a window into our subconscious mind. We generally miss what our emotions are trying to tell us because we have a tendency to make them about other people. Our emotions can also become a major distraction. Rather than focusing on the source of our negative emotions, which is our fear, we might have a tendency to focus on the person or the situation that ignited or induced the feeling of fear.

Stop spending your time, energy, and attention trying to fight back on the outside and start addressing the underlying fear itself. When you feel yourself getting angry, sad, or whatever negative emotion, remember to take note of how the situation made you feel. Address that fear in your next meditation by figuring out the source, or belief, driving that reaction.

The source is a situation from your past that made you adopt a belief that became a catalyst for the current negative emotion you are feeling. Once you find the earliest situation in which you felt that same feeling and the place where it exists in your body, then you can do the release technique. Through this process, your current negative emotions actually become the source of further internal freedom. With practice, you will reach a point where you embrace uncertainty and embrace uncomfortable situations as a means of growth.

That is true personal mastery.

THE EMOTIONAL INTEGRATION TECHNIQUE STEP-BY-STEP

- Please close your eyes and get comfortable in your chair. Now start focusing on your breathing. Bring your breath all the way down to your heart. Do this for a few minutes until you start to feel relaxed. Once you feel relaxed follow the steps below.

- Bring up an intense negative emotion that you feel on a regular basis. You can think of a situation that is a real trigger for you or, go back to a recent memory in which you were upset or angry. It can be any negative emotion, whether it's sadness, anger, frustration, contempt, or jealousy.

- Allow yourself to feel the emotions. You have to fully embrace the emotion and let it wash over you. Remember you are in a safe place, and the emotion will be gone when you are done.

- Identify where that emotion shows up in your body. It can be any-where—your throat, heart, head, back, shoulders, stomach, legs, arms, or the base of your spine.

- Feel into the pain and identify the memory that's attached to that pain. Don't think too hard. Just feel the pain and allow it to take you back to the first time this pain showed up in your life. The pain has a memory attached to it.

- Identify the fear. Determine what fear is associated with the mem-ory. Remember, you adopted the fear when you were a child; you didn't have the mental or physical capacity to defend yourself, so you adopted fear as protection.

- Ask yourself if this pain, and the associated fear, still serves you. Do you still need this fear for protection? Just know that fear is like a guard that you put on duty, and it stays in place until you release it.

- Recognize that this fear once served as a benefit to you, but now it's holding you back.

- Continue to feel the pain. In order to release it, you need to let it process. Then move love and gratitude into the pain and fear. You have to love and be grateful for the fear and the protection it offered you.

- Give love and gratitude for the version of you that adopted the fear. You were only doing the best you could. You were only trying to protect yourself. Thank and honor that version of you for its strength.

- Tell the younger version of yourself that, because of your strength, you made it and you no longer need this fear to protect you. Then release it.

- Say, "I release this fear and I choose love." Keep saying this to yourself until the pain dissipates and disappears.

- Take as much time as you need for the pain to fully release. Once it does release, notice how easily you are breathing and listen to see if you can hear the peaceful sound of white noise in your head.

- Take a deep breath and bring your presence back to the room.

YOUR MIND LIES BUT YOUR BODY ALWAYS TELLS THE TRUTH

Below is a list of various types of emotions, fears, or situations that are commonly manifested in different parts of the body. Please understand that this list is not exhaustive or absolute; any type of emotion can appear anywhere in the body. These are patterns that we observed while walking others through the process. They should prove helpful as you try to discover what is going on inside of you. Please also know that some emotions can show up in more than one area.

Heart

- betrayal
- abandonment
- heartbreak
- loss

Lower abdomen

- physical, mental, and sexual abuse
- neglect
- lack of emotional safety
- disgust
- emotional guardedness
- worry

Upper abdomen and torso

- control issues
- anger
- defensiveness
- worry
- stress
- anxiety
- embarrassment

Chest, upper torso

- anxiety
- feeling overwhelmed
- panic

Shoulders

- feeling as though you are carrying the weight of the world
- belief that your needs don't matter
- stress

Arms

- belief that life is a fight
- failure to stick up for yourself

Legs

- desire to run away
- feeling stuck in bad situations

Base of spine or lower back

- lack of physical safety
- fear of attack
- feeling scared

Throat

- belief that you don't have a voice
- feeling unheard
- concern about expressing defensiveness or anger
- failure to express your truth

Forehead

- fighting or ignoring your intuition

Brain

- confusion
- indecision

CHAPTER 17

THERE IS AN EASIER WAY: RESISTANCE VS. FLOW

FIGHT CLUB

Life is suffering. That is the one theme that most religions seem to agree on. Is it true? Is life suffering? It sure seems true, because most people are suffering on some level.

Here are other questions: "Does it have to be this way?" "Do we have to suffer through life?" "What is the cause of all this suffering?"

We don't think we have to suffer through life. We like this saying: "In life, pain is required but suffering is optional."

What is a big source of suffering? Worry! What is worry? It's a state of suffering that is the result of projecting our fears. This is what makes life feel like a fight. From the moment we adopt fear, we believe we are fighting for our survival.

There is pain in life, and we shouldn't want to deny it. Pain serves a great purpose in your life. Besides the obvious, "letting you know that something is wrong" pain, other forms of pain make all types of happiness possible. You cannot fully experience any emotion until you have experienced its opposite emotion. You can't be happy until you have felt the contrast of sadness. You can't know what light is unless you have been in the dark. We often hear people trying to wish away all the painful experiences they have had in their lives. They don't realize that, if that happened, all their good experiences would be gone as well.

Pain has never been the problem; suffering is the problem. Most people don't seem to know the difference. Pain is acute, short-term discomfort meant to alert you that something is wrong. Suffering is chronic, intense pain felt over a long period of time.

When it comes to our emotions, most of the suffering from the worries we experience in life is self-inflicted. It is the result of adopting a fear state.

FEAR STATE

What is a fear state? It is a state of mind you adopt when you get thrown into survival mode.

From that point forward, all the decisions you make have already been affected on some level by your drive for survival. This means you can't make a decision that you believe will put your survival at risk. Essentially, when you're in this state, all your decisions are made through a fear state of mind. Once you believe your survival is at stake, that becomes the first subconscious priority of your perception. When this happens, it is not a choice; it is a mandate.

Fear is the tool used by your perception to ensure your survival. Your mind will always force you to consider the risk associated with any decision you make. Here's the problem. When you are in a fear state, your mind weighs every decision against your survival. It determines whether your decision is worth putting your survival at risk. Your mind conjures up a bunch of fear to keep you from taking on any risk.

The reason you worry is because your mind believes almost every decision is a matter of life and death. If you are in a constant state of worry, it means your mind is functioning perfectly. Society would have you believe that worrying somehow makes you weak. This could not be further from the truth. If you worry, you are just standing up for your convictions.

Since you are in survival mode, your subconscious mind is always miscalculating what's at stake. The reason why life is suffering is because, in your mind, all roads lead to death. When you are in a fear state, any type of uncertainty points toward potential death. Rejection, loneliness, failure, loss, abandonment, loss of control, isolation, inadequacy, being unproductive . . . they all lead to the worst kind of suffering: an ugly, slow, extremely painful death.

It is hard to accept life in a fear state and the fact that your every decision is, in some way, influenced by fear. Here is a question that will demonstrate how much of a role fear plays in your life: "How different would you and your life be if you absolutely knew that your fears aren't real?"

Your mind is probably spinning with endless possibilities. You probably feel your life would be so different and you would be so much more. Like nothing could hold you back.

The fact that you clearly understand that your life would be different shows you are, in fact, living in a fear state. You intuitively see that, on some level, fear is dictating your decisions. Otherwise, your answer to the question would be that nothing would change and life would be exactly as it is now.

How much is fear influencing the life you are living? Consider how different your life would be without fear. If it would be dramatically different, then you are living in a significant amount of fear. If it would be slightly different, then you are living in a little bit of fear. If you believe it would be almost the same, then you're probably lying to yourself.

The minute you choose to adopt a fear, it becomes real to you even if you're not consciously aware of it. When you believe your fears are real, you spend a lot of time combating or defending against them. What's really ironic is, your attempts to defend yourself against fear are exactly what creates the conditions for that fear to manifest in your life.

We are still embracing our ancient, outdated fears concerning survival, and that is creating the very conditions that put our survival at risk, through wars, starvation, and environmental problems.

Fear is not the problem. Fear's only job is to protect you. The real problem is living in fear. The only reason you would need to live in the fear state would be if your life was constantly in danger. How often is your actual survival really at stake? Unless you live where there is famine or in a war-torn part of the world, the answer for most people is "very rarely or never." But you wouldn't know that from the nightly news. The media makes you worry that your life is always in jeopardy. The fear state is probably why we are so obsessed with the negative to begin with. Our fixation on negative information and bad news only exacerbates the problem.

Why does any of this matter? It doesn't if you don't mind a lifetime full of suffering. Worrying robs your life of the happiness and joy you deserve. This is what really started to wear on us. Even though we were getting everything we wanted in life, we were not able to enjoy it. We were in a constant state of fear, driving ourselves into a constant state of anxiety.

GO WITH THE FLOW STATE

Eventually we realized that life does not have to feel like a fight. We realized we could move into a flow state. You don't have to take our word for it. The evidence can be found in your own life.

Have you ever thought about why some things in life come easy and others are hard? You probably chalk it up to luck or skills or genetics or intelligence. Most people are not stuck in survival mode in every area of their lives. You can be in a fear state in one area of your life and a flow state in another.

You only fight when you're in fear. When you take the fear out of the equation, there is only flow. Fear is the resistance you feel as you move toward the things you are uncertain about. Once those fears are lifted and you move into flow, resistance also goes away.

Consider this: If you could go back ten years in time and tell yourself just one thing, what's the most valuable advice you could give yourself? We have put a lot of thought into this. We believe there is only one thing you could say to yourself that would have any real impact on the quality of your life: "You are going to have some ups and downs, but everything is going to work out for you, so please stop worrying and enjoy the journey."

Now let's do the same thing going ten years into the future. If the 'you' ten years from now could come back and say just one thing, what would it be? It would be the exact same advice. Since time travel does not seem likely in our lifetime, don't wait for a visit from your future self to stop worrying and enjoy the journey!

How do you move away from fear and resistance into flow?

You have to change the information you use to decide the direction of your life. When you start from a place of fear, you will end up in a place of fear. Fear and flow cannot coexist. It is impossible to access flow from a place of fear. When you move into a flow state you have access to new information. New results come from new information. It can't be any other way.

You can't have the same results with different information—that's impossible. Once you are different, the world can only meet you where you are. It all starts by questioning the lie of fear and becoming something different.

This is why life is not about doing, it's about becoming. Most people believe they get paid for doing, but this is fundamentally wrong. If it were true, and the many flaws in the system were removed, everyone who is doing the same job would be paid the same amount of money. All things considered, if two people with very similar backgrounds do the same job and the same amount of work, they should make the same amount of money, right? Wrong.

Inevitably, one person will bring more value to the position than the other person and, as a result, will get paid more. Who decides your value? You do. Most of the people who have worked for us over the years mistakenly believed that we decided their value, but we didn't. Only you can decide your value, and it's based on what you believe about yourself. It is the one thing that shines through once the talking stops and the work begins. The world will always adhere to your value, regardless of where you start. Over time, those around you will see your value, good or bad.

Remember that the outside always matches the inside. The only thing you should care about is finding an opportunity to demonstrate your value. James once heard someone say, "If you get paid for what you do, you make a living. If you get paid for who you are, you make a fortune." If you think about it, this makes perfect sense. When you get paid for what you do and what you do goes away, then so does your ability to make money. When who you are has value, you have that value wherever you go.

How do you determine your value? It's a great question and one that depends on a number of factors. We all have the same amount of intrinsic value, it's just that some of us recognize our value more than others. It's easy to ignore your value, just as it's easy to ignore your gifts. Let's begin by exploring what makes you unique.

Do you know what makes you unique? It's probably not what you think. Most people assume it is some trait or talent, but no matter what talents you have, there are other people who share those same talents. The only thing that is truly unique about you is your story, your perspective. No two lives are exactly the same and no one else has your knowledge or understanding of the world. Your story is yours and yours alone. Your story has great value.

If you wake up to the truth about yourself, you're in a position right now to help shape humanity's viewpoint through your unique perspective. It's time to embrace your power and stop living in the delusion of fear. When you have to courage to stand up and recognize your unique value, you give others permission to do the same.

Most of the information we are sharing with you in this book did not come from our education or from reading other books. These ideas came from our efforts to understand our experiences and our attempts to understand our unique stories and perspectives. Now we are sharing them with you.

The world does not need any more parrots. It needs people who have the courage to stand up and own their shit. People who explore their unique perspectives help everyone come to a deeper understanding of what it means to be human. Evolution is life and life is evolution. For the first time in history, we have the opportunity to consciously evolve past our biggest adversary: living in fear. To do this, we must have the courage to acknowledge our fear, own our story, and use our gifts and talents to share our unique perspective with the world.

Your value comes from understanding you are good enough just as you are, even if it is not currently reflected in your outside circumstances. If you don't feel like you are good enough, it's because you believe the lie that happened when you suffered your first major rejection. That lie has become your truth and the truth now seems like a lie.

Here is an example of how this works. Imagine a child is walking across a schoolyard and someone shouts, "Hey, you're fat and ugly!" The child pauses and considers what was just said to them. They think, "Am I fat and ugly?" If in that moment the child chooses to accept that information as truth, they suffer their first major rejection and an identity crisis unfolds as we described in chapter 5. The child becomes very insecure about his looks and body. This insecurity moves him toward an unhealthy relationship with food.

Fast-forward 30 years, and this person is now an adult. He was once a perfectly normal-looking, average-size child, but is now what most people would consider fat and not very good looking. The lie now seems to be true, and the truth now seems like a lie. You're probably thinking it is true, he is fat and ugly. The lie that altered his life was the belief he adopted as a child. The words that people told him about being fat and ugly did not create the problem; it was the fact that he chose to believe them and make them true.

The belief that he isn't good enough wasn't true back then, and it's still not true, no matter what he currently sees in the mirror. There must be some deeper meaning to this trauma. The deeper meaning is, of course, the introduction to fear. From that point forward, everything in their life became a product of fear. We like to think that fear only plays a small role in our lives, but that couldn't be further from the truth. Fear becomes our life when we adopt a fear state of mind.

Fear State

When you're in a fear state, it's all about control. You don't want any surprises. You always want to know the answer. You want to control the narrative and the outcome of all the circumstances surrounding every situation you're in.

Your survival depends on your being right all the time. Any risk you take has to be calculated, and you are always playing defense. You fully understand that you're in this alone and you cannot afford to be wrong. The only person you can depend on is you.

Flow State

When you're a flow state, you learn to embrace uncertainty. It's all about questions. You love surprises. You are open to being wrong. You fully expect the narrative to change as information and circumstances change.

Creativity depends on your ability to question everything. Risk is a welcome part of the process. You can't afford to stay stagnant. You remain open to receiving help from outside sources because you understand that you can't do it alone.

PARASYMPATHETIC SAY WHAT?

Fear has a physiological side in connection to your autonomic nervous system, which controls the functions in your body that occur automatically. Part of this system deals with fear, specifically your fight-or-flight responses. Your autonomic nervous system is broken up into two separate parts: the parasympathetic state and the sympathetic state. The explanation below is an oversimplification, but we feel this is something very important to understand. We encourage you to do further research in this area.

At any given moment, you are either in the parasympathetic state or the sympathetic state. With a few minor exceptions, this is an either-or scenario. Here's how to distinguish between the two: When you are in a parasympathetic state, you are in a calm, mindful space of rest or homeostasis. When you are in a sympathetic state, you are in a heightened, active condition of stress. This is a fight-or-flight response to a perceived threat or when your body moves into an active state such as rigorous exercise. In sympathetic mode, your bodily functions change in order to prepare for the threat or activity. Your heart rate increases to move more blood into your extremities to run or fight. Almost every function of the body is affected, including your digestive system, lungs, throat, adrenals, stomach, and even your sex organs. Your body slows the function of some things in order to give more power to others. Think of it as similar to the turbocharger function of your car when you stomp on the accelerator. It gives you extra power when you need it. It's like when Scotty on *Star Trek* diverts all auxiliary power to the thrusters.

When your system is functioning in a healthy way, there is a gentle dance between the two sides. When you spend too much time in a sympathetic state, it causes major dysfunction in the mind and body. The main reason is our emotions. Our bodies and minds did not evolve to differentiate between physical and emotional attacks. Our mind views them both as attacks and switches into the sympathetic state. This causes us to spend far too much time in turbocharge mode.

Anytime we feel scared, stressed, anxious, embarrassed, or nervous, we are in a system that was only meant to be used periodically. When we are in this state, we are stealing energy from all other body functions. Stimulants, such as caffeine, also move us from a parasympathetic state to a sympathetic state.

Do you ever wake up feeling more tired than when you went to bed? We've all been there. Why does this happen? Our bodies are supposed to repair themselves when we sleep, right? During sleep, the body uses blood glucose as fuel to repair itself. The more we are in a sympathetic state during the day, the less our bodies are able to repair themselves when we sleep. Therein lies the problem.

The solution is to take control of this system. How do you do that? When you are feeling stressed or anxious, take a few minutes to do heart-based deep breathing, a kind of micro meditation. If we use the example of running from a predator, when the threat is gone you stop running and catch your breath. You breathe deeply and calm yourself down. You send a signal to the brain to shift back to homeostasis. The system works this way because, when you are in fight-or-flight, the body moves into a total reactionary mode and basically loses connection with the brain. Fortunately, as we've agreed, we are rarely in a life-threatening situation. If we can realize this, we can use the deep breathing to send a signal to our body and brain to switch back to a parasympathetic state.

Starting and ending your day with a short meditation, combined with regular exercise, can bring amazing benefits. If you are having trouble with sleep, weight, digestion, thyroid, cortisol, energy levels, blood pressure, or many other issues, understanding how this works will help you better manage and take control of your life.

THE RESISTANCE VS. FLOW QUIZ

This is an easy tool to show you which parts of your life are naturally in flow and which parts are naturally in fear. Below is a sample list of different aspects of life. Get a pen or a pencil, and as you read through this list one item at a time, say whichever word (RESISTANCE or FLOW) first comes to mind and mark the appropriate category.

ASPECT OF LIFE	RESISTANCE	FLOW
Romantic relationships		
Friendships		
Work		
Children		
Marriage		
Dating		
School		
Health		
Fitness		
Writing		
Reading		
Sports		
Art		
Music		
Public speaking		
Caring about what others think		
Social media		

MR. CHAOS AND MRS. ORDER

We want to propose an idea to you. What if chaos and order were used to name the opposite ends of a scale to describe people's personalities? Some people thrive in chaos and others in order. One is not better than the other, they are just different. People who thrive on the order side of things are masters of execution. Just give them clear goals, guidelines, and objectives and they will make shit happen. People who thrive on the chaos side of things enjoy moving into uncertainty and embracing the unknown to try and put all the broken pieces together. Give them a problem and they will solve it. Then there are those who are in between. They may prefer one side or the other but are capable in both.

Where do you fall on the scale? Now think of everyone you know and place them somewhere along the scale. When we did this exercise, our world and everyone in it started to make a lot more sense. Here is the crazy thing, if you are firmly on one side or the other, you likely have been made to feel guilty for your lack of talent, creativity, organization, execution, problem solving, or commitment. You were not like the person sitting across from you who was expecting you to be like them. Understanding this should also help you to know why people fail to live up to your expectations. It is because you often ask people to do things they are actually not capable of doing. They are just not wired that way.

We often classify people as failures simply because they can't be someone they are not. This also impacts the way we communicate with one another. People who prefer order also like to communicate in orderly ways. They want to summarize and get to a clear conclusion. People who prefer chaos like to theorize and to leave things open-ended. People who prefer order are planners who thrive in routine. People who prefer chaos like to go with the flow and see what happens.

No matter which side of this scale you fall on, when you're expected, or forced, to the other side, it becomes a terrible experience and can be soul crushing. When you start looking at people through this lens, stop expecting them to be what they're not, and start leveraging them for what they are. This is where the magic happens. It is important to know that it is possible to be one way in part of your life and another way in other parts of your life. Complete dysfunction comes when you get extreme about your view and get so invested in it that you don't understand the value of the other side.

For us, this was a very hard lesson to learn, because James is Mr. Chaos and Steph is Mrs. Order. By learning this lesson, we were able to move away from our misplaced expectations into a deeper place of love and gratitude for each other. We are also able to help each other to strengthen the side we are not naturally drawn to. James definitely needs more order in his life and Steph helps facilitate that for him. She still lets him have his chaos as long as it doesn't drift too far out of his office or closet. Steph needs to learn to go with the flow a little more and James is able to move her in that direction as well—as long as it doesn't involve James deciding what time they should be at an airport.

The important takeaway is that the ability to deal at both ends of the spectrum is necessary in order for you to thrive and grow. Both tendencies have equal value in the system. Understanding this is key to getting the most out of your relationships, career pursuits, health, fitness, time. It is a huge part of understanding your strengths and weaknesses and those of the people around you.

PART SIX

THE ONLY WAY OUT IS THROUGH ... HELPING OTHERS

CHAPTER

18

UNDERSTANDING THE POWER OF YOUR STORY

STEPH: *YOU'RE CRAZY IF THINK I AM TELLING MY STORY*

Vulnerability for me always equaled weakness. I was so terrified from my abuse that I thought if I told my parents, they wouldn't believe me and somehow I would be rejected if I spoke my truth. So I made a conscious effort to "keep it together": keep my feelings inside, never show emotions, not overreact, and keep my story hidden from the world.

I thought men wanted women who were strong and didn't show emotions. I didn't want to show the emotions I was feeling inside. It was so easy for me to put up my walls after my sexual abuse. In my relationships, I didn't allow anyone to see the real me. I didn't tell them I was sad, lonely, or felt broken inside. I seemed to find people whofelt the same way about themselves, and it always ended up being very chaotic and painful.

When I met James and he shared his story with me, I was shocked and sad for him. But I never saw the openness he displayed as weakness. It actually gave me the courage to share my story. He told me that it wasn't my fault, and that I had to stop blaming myself for all the abuse and for my dad leaving. It hit me like a ton of bricks when he said it wasn't my fault. I felt distress about having kept it all inside me. How could I expect anyone to tell me it wasn't my fault if I didn't tell my story? I will save you the trouble and tell you right now that if you have gone through abuse, IT ISN'T YOUR FAULT. The only part of it that is your fault is the false narrative that you chose to believe about yourself because of it. If you're going to tell your story and be vulnerable, find someone you can trust who will create a soft place to land, as James did for me. We were two sad souls who connected through our stories. Maybe not everyone will get you or connect to your story, but that doesn't mean you have to hide who you are because of it. James and I have always accepted each other, flaws and all.

When we were planning our first Powerful U event for helping other people, we initially wanted to get the most impactful speakers we could find. One day James came home from work and said, "I have an idea and you're not going to like it." I thought, "Oh no, what has he planned now?" He said, "I think we should film our personal stories to show at the event and tie it all to the speakers' content in order to make the most impact." A thousand flashes of nightmares came screaming into my head as I thought, "Oh hell no, he must be joking!" We had only shared some of our stories with close family and friends, but now we were going to announce this to the world? I was dying right then and there. I had never been on film before. I hated the sound of my voice. How was I going to sit in front of a film crew and share my story? What made it worse was knowing that this film was going to be shared with the world at the event. I was just praying and hoping no one would reject me. My nightmare had come true.

Being vulnerable turned out to be the thing I was most afraid of. I had felt safe enough to share my story with James, but not with thousands of strangers. As hard as it was to film my story, I walked out of the studio afterward and the sun was shining and I threw my hands up in the air. I felt free. I had let it out and I felt at peace.

When event time came, once again I was thrown into fear. I was backstage with James when the videos played, and it was hard. I fell into the trap of worrying about what others would think of me. During the rest of the event, it blew my mind how many people came up and thanked me for being vulnerable enough to share my story. They said I gave them the courage they needed to stop being ashamed of their past and to share their story. This was one of the most humbling experiences of my life. I never dreamed something as simple as sharing your story could make such an impact on so many people's lives.

This hit me on a much deeper level when, a couple of weeks after the event, my brother asked me to lunch. He is two years older than I am and we were close as children before the divorce. We played together all the time, but when we moved and our lives were uprooted, we both became angry and distant. It wasn't until we were adults that we became close again. I wasn't at all prepared for what he told me at lunch that day. He said he had gone home from the event and shared his story for the first time with his wife of seventeen years. He shared with me that he had been molested when he was eight years old by a family member. Added to that was the pain he felt because our dad had left us. Those burdens made him feel suicidal at various times through the years. He had put a gun in his mouth several times and contemplated pulling the trigger.

I was speechless and stared at him in shock. This entire time we could have had each other's back, but instead we had both suffered alone in silence. It was a very powerful moment as we both realized we weren't the only ones hiding in shame.

The ones you love the most may be the ones who need your story the most. Vulnerability equals strength, not weakness. Don't let fear keep you from sharing your story. Don't isolate yourself or worry about being judged. So many of us think that vulnerability is power—unless we are the ones being vulnerable. You are as powerful as you believe you are. Let your story out and free yourself from your own personal prison. Your story only has power over you if you keep it a secret.

JAMES: *THIS SHIT IS EMBARRASSING*

The reason I didn't want to tell my story was not about vulnerability. After all, I had freely shared my past with Steph. For me, it was embarrassing. I didn't want to be judged for being a former drug addict who had served time in jail.

Over the years, I had shared my background with only a few close friends. When we started Powerful U, the hardest part for me was knowing I would have to tell this story. It wasn't that I thought people would reject me, it was hard because I had disconnected from my victim story. I cringed at the idea of picking it back up and making that narrative a part of my life again. Worst of all, I had to sit down and have a long talk with our older children. I had planned on telling them eventually, but I hated feeling that I was, in a sense, being forced to do it much sooner.

Filming our stories for the event was way less painful for me than it was for Steph. I took comfort in knowing that almost everyone loves a comeback story. Unlike Steph, I knew that our stories would have an impact on people. I just had no idea how much. After our stories played at the event, we went upstairs to have lunch. When we had finished eating, I told Steph I was going to run to the restroom and that I would meet her backstage. I had just finished washing my hands and I turned around to see a man standing there. He looked at me and said, "Dude, I have to give you a hug." I must admit, that was the first time I had ever hugged a stranger in a bathroom. I don't know what happens in women's restrooms, but there is no hugging in the men's. As I exited into the main area, people started stopping me to thank me for sharing my story. Then they wanted to share their stories with me. As a small crowd began to form around me, I looked up and saw Steph also surrounded by people. I met up with her and, as we stood together, even more people came up and started sharing their stories with us. It was incredible how much love and encouragement these total strangers showed us. It made me realize that everybody has a story and that these stories have great power to help us identify and connect with each other.

STEPH & JAMES: *IT'S YOUR TURN*

What we didn't fully comprehend until later was that we had given people permission to tell their stories. As you open up and embrace and share your past, it will create opportunities for you to connect more deeply with those around you. In doing so, you will help people realize they are not alone. This then gives them permission to share their stories with others as well.

Our hope is that sharing our story will become a movement where people are no longer living in fear of their past. Then we can all stop focusing on our differences and start celebrating our similarities. As people start opening up to one another, it will change lives and, eventually, the power of vulnerability will shift people's hearts and minds all across the globe.

POWERFUL U

WE KEPT OUR PROMISE

When James was in that jail cell, he made a promise to himself. He decided that if he ever did find the answers about how to consciously create his life, he would not keep it to himself; he would share it with others. When he met Steph, she felt the same way. Steph wanted to reach people who were dealing with the same type of emotional pain she was dealing with and offer them the help she had never received. Powerful U is us keeping our promise to give back.

Powerful U is the world's first personal evolution company.

MISSION STATEMENT

We are seekers who find the state of humanity inadequate. We believe the unrealized potential of the individual is both the source of and solution to this problem. Our goal is to help inspire fellow seekers to tap into their own unlimited potential through a personalized combination of philosophy, science, technology, and community.

OUR DEFINITION OF
PERSONAL EVOLUTION

Personal evolution is the process of shifting your perception by removing the contradicting thoughts, beliefs, and actions that stand between who you are now and who you want to become.

A PASSION PROJECT

We always felt that the self-help industry was lacking certain essential qualities. When it came to attendance at events aimed at providing the information required to undergo personal growth, getting the best knowledge seemed to be a "pay to play" game. In order to evolve and improve your life, you had to spend a lot of money to get access to the information and the experts.

We realize the entire self-help industry can't all be nonprofit, but we feel much of the industry operates counterintuitively. Most self-help enterprises seem focused on generating revenue over helping anyone and everyone regardless of their status or financial standing in life.

It seemed the industry had chosen to focus only on reaching those who had the financial means to participate, and this was reflected in the demographics of the people who attended these events. Most of the industry went upstream instead of downstream, ignoring the vast majority of people who may not have the money or resources to access information they sorely needed.

We believe that if you have the desire to grow, you should have access to the information and the people you need to make growth possible. There are more than enough books on self-help and personal growth, but most are too vague, too unrealistic, too idealistic, or they lack the practical substance necessary to show you how to grow and evolve on your own.

There are thousands of books and concepts out there. With the internet and social media, a lot more information is readily available. The problem is, anyone with a cell phone can present themselves as an expert. Most of what you find online is recycled tips and tricks. Much of the information is based on guesswork and not founded on solid principles. We are grateful you stumbled onto this book and we hope it helps you.

With that in mind, we decided to disrupt the status quo of the self-help industry and flip it on its head. We decided to help individuals realize they can be their own guru. We have always wanted to help people, but we knew that we had to learn the answers for ourselves first. You teach what you learn. One of our teachers told us this, and we thought that was counterintuitive. My dream was to facilitate people in achieving their own dreams, not just mimicking others. We wanted to figure out the path to achieving personal success, track what it took to get there, and then explain it to people in a language that was too easy to ignore and too simple to misunderstand.

It amazed us that so many of the teachers of things like the law of attraction were unhealthy and broke. Many people seem to think enlightenment comes by chance, but we knew that if we found it, in whatever form, we would want to share it with others.

We reverse-engineered our success back to perceptions and how we are truly the creators of our experiences; not in a woo-woo esoteric way, but rather in a practical way that can be tracked and replicated. Our idea for the creation of Powerful U was our effort to give back.

A few years ago, we started tossing around ideas for the content of Powerful U, and when we sold our software company, we officially launched Powerful U in April of 2017.

When we designed Powerful U, we initially conceived it as an internet and social media content company to enable us to develop self-help ideas into podcasts and videos that we would post on platforms such as YouTube. As we moved forward we realized that a lot of people were doing this already, filling the niche we had identified. So we sharpened our focus.

It was never our intention to tell our own personal stories as a part of the event, or the book, or the movie. In fact, we were embarrassed about our stories. As we moved toward our first event, we realized the only way to make it significantly different was to figure out a way for people to identify with the content through the telling of personal stories. We hoped this approach would open people up so they could see aspects of themselves through our own journey. The fundamental principle we teach is to reach for the largest opportunity and then engage with the uncertainty around that.

We decided to hold an event called "Evolve Your Perception." We brought in dynamic, well-known speakers like our friend Beau Lotto and many others. Our first seminar attracted more than 2,500 people to Salt Lake City during November 2018. It was, by any stretch of the imagination, a huge hit with everyone involved. Our goal for the event was to give every person who attended a chance to experience their own paradigm shift. Judging by the tremendous feedback we received, we feel like we accomplished most of our objectives.

We knew from the beginning of Powerful U that we eventually wanted to affect the lives of billions of people. Once we wrote the content for the event, it became apparent that we had the basis for creating a book and for filming a movie. We continue to hold live events and we are moving into expanding our presence on the Internet. All this, along with the book and movie, will propel our vision forward.

Our mission at Powerful U remains simple and straightforward, to help you as an individual empower yourself to create the life you most desire, using our personalized tools and engaging content. We are all about meeting you where you're at, and then getting you where you need to go.

We invite you to learn more at www.powerful-u.com

THIS IS
THE BEGINNING,
NOT THE END

IS IT WORTH IT?

Most people want to hear about our successes, but few want to hear about the sacrifices we made in order to get to where we are. Evolution, by its very nature, requires sacrifices. Many people are looking for an elevator to the top of the mountain, but that elevator doesn't exist. You have to climb every step. And the higher you go, the steeper and harder it gets.

We always laugh when we hear people say things like, "I want to be rich." When we ask why, they usually respond by saying they want to be comfortable. It's funny because that has never been our experience. Achieving our dreams is all about being uncomfortable and embracing levels of uncertainty that we never thought possible. We can't strive for a goal of comfort when the path leading there is all about facing uncertainty.

Our initial sacrifices were to give up the distracting activities that everyone else seemed to be engaging in. James would go to work and talk to people who said they played video games until two in the morning. Well, who has the time for that? We wouldn't be watching a Netflix series either, because we were talking and discussing issues in the evening.

Instead of going out to clubs, or concerts, or restaurants at night, we were staying home working on our journey.

We just wanted to figure out why we felt the way we did. We wanted to get rid of all the sadness and anger we had inside. We had to keep asking ourselves what we wanted more, to spend our days worrying about other people's lives or to spend our time investing in us.

As we worked on ourselves, health and fitness became a big part of our journey. We knew if we didn't feel well or have energy, we would never reach our full potential. We knew we needed to figure out this piece if we were ever going to become the best versions of ourselves. We no longer live in a world where the effects of diet on the body are a mystery. We stopped ignoring our contradictions in this area and set out to find our optimal state of health. We realized that adopting a healthy diet, an exercise routine, and a daily meditation practice were critical elements of success.

It's important to understand that there is a level of commitment and work that goes into any improvement process. You're doomed to fail if your body and mind can't support you in your goals. Too often people fool themselves about what it's going to take to achieve their dreams. You need to understand that it's hard. We don't say this to discourage you; but you need to understand the sacrifice it's going to take.

This journey requires everything you have. If you go into it thinking anything less, you're never going to make it. We want to give reasonable expectations for what you're going to face as you embark on, or continue, your journey.

The longer we walked down this path, the more we realized we were not approaching the end, but the beginning. Once we learned how to create our existence and peel back the emotional trauma that had been holding us back our entire lives, we started to realize that the only real limit in life is time. The vast majority of us waste our most precious commodity. So here is the final thing that differentiated us from everyone else we knew—we seemed to have a greater sense of urgency about everything we did. We find that most of the people we meet who are extremely successful have that sense of urgency as well. This makes sense from the perspective of perception. When we have a sense of urgency, it demonstrates we have moved past the "wanting and trying to believe stage," and into the "knowing and experiencing" phase. It means we are way more likely to see opportunities, decide to seize them, and take action. Just like everything else we have been talking about, having a sense of urgency can be difficult at times. How do we manage it all? As with everything else, it comes down to asking the right questions.

The big question is not whether or not the journey is hard, but whether it's worth it. We can promise you from everything we've been through, and from the life we live today, that it is worth it.

WHAT NOW?

There are a few ideas we would like to share with you as we come to the end of this journey together. As you move forward with implementing the ideas in this book, things in your life will begin to shift rapidly. Please understand that this can be very unsettling. Be patient and loving with yourself and know that these changes mean you are making progress. Stand tall as your fears and insecurities assault you faster than you can imagine. Remind yourself that the fear is a lie and that everything you are experiencing is literally in your mind. Know that you are safe. The way out is through processing these fears one by one.

Everyone in your life, especially those closest to you, will be changed by your journey in some way. Often, as you face your fears, they will spill out over the people you love. This can be difficult for them and hard for you. We found that keeping a very open dialogue with the people around us helped them know what we were going through. We found that this vulnerability fostered a new level of respect for each other and helped those around us, especially our five children. It helped them better understand us and realize how to live their own lives on a much deeper level.

The most important thing you have to know moving forward is that it's impossible to make this journey alone. You are going to need support along the way. The question is, how do you get the help that you need? Well, by helping others, of course. Wait, what? Remember when we said that success is all about asking the right questions? We live in a world where most people are asking, "What can you do for me?" This is the wrong question. The right question is, "What can I do for you?" True success only comes through serving others. In other words, you can only get what you want out of life by helping others to get what they want.

Demanding the respect of others is not leadership, it's fear. Real leaders are the ones whose first objective is to serve and who influence others to do the same.

Most people are good, with good intentions. Yet they falsely believe it is necessary to *have* in order to give. The reverse is actually true. You have to give in order to have. You don't give the most because you have the most, you have the most because you give the most. And no matter how much or how little you have, you always have something to give, because it's not just about money. You can give kindness, love, gratitude, a helping hand, or your most valuable resource: time.

Here is where most of us get stuck. We get so hyperfocused on ourselves that we literally forget about the people around us and fail to see their needs. The question is, why? It's because we concentrate on the wrong things, mostly our own pain and struggles. If you smash your finger in a car door, it's hard to think about anything other than the pain in your finger. Emotional pain and struggles work the same way. It is very easy to get stuck when you're focusing on your own pain. The quickest way to break through this is to take your focus off yourself and put it on helping someone else. Why is this so important? It's based on a principle we discussed in this book, that you get more of the things you focus on. If it's your own pains, struggles, or fears, you get more of those. When you move your focus toward helping others, in acts of love and kindness, you get more love and kindness. You are shifting your attention from the things you don't want to the things you do want. When you provide more opportunities for others, you create more for yourself. When you help other people find solutions for their problems, you learn how to better solve your own problems because your focus has shifted from problems to solutions. Looking at someone else's life and problems also makes it easier to be more objective about your own and to see solutions. You get what you give. It literally can't be any other way.

True giving means doing it without any expectation of getting something in return. Giving with expectations is your ego seeking validation through the act of giving. This turns giving into a fear-based activity, which will have the opposite effect in your life. If you give from a place of fear, you will get more fear in return. Admittedly, giving freely with no expectation can be hard. As you start giving more freely and openly, you will find that your capacity to give will quickly outpace other individuals' capacity to receive. Then your ego will not get validation from your giving, leading to thoughts that the recipients are ungrateful. This is not usually the case. Most people just don't know how to react to the level of love and kindness you are expressing with no strings attached, because they have never experienced anything like it. Placing an expectation on giving creates another pattern or loop that will trap you.

What you give truly does come back to you tenfold, but almost never from the people you give to, or in the same form or manner in which it was given. It is often manifest in what seems like a totally unrelated way or circumstance. Mastering the art of giving freely, with no expectations, will transform your life faster than any other factor. We look forward to sharing in your journey and seeing what you become.

RESOURCES

The overarching theme of this book is to question everything. It was never meant to be the be-all and end-all of information. It was only meant to be the start of a new conversation that you have with yourself and others. You should start questioning everything all the time, including everything you have read in this book. Remember, life is not about finding answers; it's about asking the right questions. In this section we have included some reference material for you on the science and studies that support various concepts and ideas we discuss in the book.

THE SCIENCE BEHIND PERCEPTION

Any consideration of the science behind human perception needs to begin with the work of Beau Lotto, PhD, and professor of neuroscience at the University of London and a visiting scholar at New York University.

In his book *Deviate: The Creative Power of Transforming Your Perception*, Dr. Lotto examines how human perception operates, showing how perception is the foundation of human experience and that each of us has it within our power to create new ways of seeing ourselves and the world. He presents in the book a series of perceptual illusions and puzzles to illustrate how easily our brains are fooled when we rely on preprogrammed assumptions.

Versions of reality we humans operate from have nothing to do with what actually exists in the physical realm. "We don't see reality," writes Lotto. "We only see what was useful to see in the past. Our species has been so successful not in spite of our inability to see reality but because of it." Lotto *further states*:

> Perception matters because it underpins everything we think, know and believe. Our sense of self, our most essential way of understanding existence, begins and ends with perception. The death that we all fear is less the death of the body and more the death of perception. Yet most of us don't know how or why our brain evolved to perceive the way it does.

Lotto *adds*:

> The brain doesn't just sit inside your skull; it sits in an interaction between what's inside your skull and its body, and the body in the world. That's where perception lives. We often forget, especially in the contemporary digital world, that we evolved in this body, in this body in this world, and that's where the brain makes meaning. Perception is in the space between.

Lotto thinks the next greatest human innovation will be a way of seeing that enables us to question all the assumptions we have inherited from our culture and our evolutionary ancestors. A key step is "to know what those assumptions are and accept them. We have to reveal them to ourselves and to others, which is the power of groups. The power of diversity, exploration, and traveling is that it reveals your assumptions to yourself."

We must learn to choose our delusions carefully, and we also need to celebrate doubt and not remain mired in certainty. "The basis of creativity is humility and not knowing. Nothing interesting comes from knowing—it comes from not knowing. It doesn't come from confidence—it comes from courage. To ask a question is scary and potentially very dangerous:

to challenge what you assumed to be true already—especially about yourself—and to question your own identity. That's the ultimate uncertainty."

SCIENCE BEHIND MINDSET

Carol Dweck, PhD, a professor of psychology at Stanford University, pioneered the idea of a person's mindset being a determining factor in whether they will experience success or failure in life.

In her book *Mindset: The New Psychology of Success,* Dr. Dweck examines how we have two types of mindsets (beliefs)—fixed and growth—which impact our perceptions and how we learn and solve problems. She also explores how our conscious and unconscious thoughts produce beliefs that influence whether we will or won't achieve our goals in life. She has been a pioneer researcher in the field of human motivation, showing why some people succeed and others don't, and teaching how to cultivate a growth mindset from an early age to foster success.

In simplified form, her idea is that some people believe their basic abilities—their talents and intelligence—are fixed traits they are born with, whereas people with a growth mindset understand that persistence, effort, and learning shape their talents and abilities and that anyone can improve if they apply themselves. Dweck produced research evidence that a growth mindset results in an ability to rebound from setbacks and learn from them while enhancing a person's chances of experiencing success and happiness. As Dweck writes about success in *Mindset*:

> We often see books with titles like *The Ten Secrets of the World's Most Successful People* crowding the shelves of bookstores, and these books may give many useful tips. But they're usually a list of unconnected pointers, like 'Take more risks!' or 'Believe in yourself!' While you're left admiring people who can do that, it's never clear how these things fit together or how you could ever become that way. So you're inspired for a few days, but basically, the world's most successful people still have their secrets.

Dweck *further states*:

> Instead, as you begin to understand the fixed and growth mindsets, you will see exactly how one thing leads to another—how a belief that your qualities are carved in stone leads to a host of thoughts and actions, and how a belief that your qualities can be cultivated leads to a host of different thoughts and actions, taking you down an entirely different road.

BENEFITS OF MEDITATION

Stilling your mind chatter to access the serenity within you is one purpose of a meditation practice. Meditation is also a tool designed to bring clarity of mind while improving self-mastery and self-knowledge.

Some widely practiced types of meditation include: Mindfulness, Transcendental, Vipassana, Loving-Kindness, and Kundalini. Each uses a somewhat different approach, but the key to most is to keep the mind's attention focused on breathing, or on repeating a mantra or a rhythmic sound such as *om*.

Regular meditation can give more clarity to the mind and the thoughts it generates, which in turn helps with the process of identifying the underlying assumptions that shape our misguided perceptions of ourselves and others. The benefits to mental and physical health ascribed to meditation are wide-ranging.

Here are examples of scientific studies affirming these benefits on mental and physical health.

The Neuroscience of Meditation: Classification, Phenomenology, Correlates, and Mechanisms

Brandmeyer T,. et al. *Progress in Brain Research*. 2019.

"Rising from its contemplative and spiritual traditions, the science of meditation has seen huge growth over the last 30 years. There is a growing body of evidence demonstrating positive benefits from meditation in some clinical populations especially for stress reduction, anxiety, depression, and pain improvement. Meditation research continues to grow, allowing us to understand greater nuances of how meditation works and its effects.

"Clinicians should be aware that meditation programs can result in small to moderate reductions of multiple negative dimensions of psychological stress. Thus, clinicians should be prepared to talk with their patients about the role that a meditation program could have in addressing psychological stress."

Modeling the Impact of Transcendental Meditation on Stroke Incidence and Mortality

Ambavane RA, et al. *Journal of Stroke and Cerebrovascular Diseases.* March 2019.

"Meditation has shown promise in clinical trials in reducing systolic blood pressure, one of the main risk factors for stroke. We aim to estimate the potential benefits of popularizing meditation on stroke incidence and mortality in the United States (U.S.).

"We used the population simulation model to estimate the effects of meditation intervention on the number of stroke cases and deaths over a course of 15 years. Our results show that we could avert nearly 200,000 stroke cases and 50,000 stroke-related deaths over the course of 15 years. Our sensitivity analysis reveals that most of the benefits come from applying the intervention for individuals older than 60 years. In addition, meditation acceptance and adherence rate play a critical role in its effectiveness.

"The practice of meditation, if properly utilized along with the regular antihypertensive medication, could substantially alleviate the burden of stroke in the U.S."

Meditation and Cardiovascular Risk Reduction: A Scientific Statement from the American Heart Association

Levine GN, et al. *Journal of the American Heart Association.* September 2017.

"Despite numerous advances in the prevention and treatment of atherosclerosis, cardiovascular disease remains a leading cause of morbidity and mortality. Novel and inexpensive interventions that can contribute to the primary and secondary prevention of cardiovascular disease are of interest. Numerous studies have reported on the benefits of meditation. Meditation instruction and practice is widely accessible and inexpensive and may thus be a potential attractive cost-effective adjunct to more traditional medical therapies. Accordingly, this American Heart Association scientific statement systematically reviewed the data on the potential benefits of meditation on cardiovascular risk.

"Neurophysiological and neuroanatomical studies demonstrate that meditation can have long-standing effects on the brain, which provide some biological plausibility for beneficial consequences on the physiological basal state and on cardiovascular risk. Studies of the effects of meditation on cardiovascular risk have included those investigating physiological response to stress, smoking cessation, blood pressure reduction, insulin resistance and metabolic syndrome, endothelial function, inducible myocardial ischemia, and primary and secondary prevention of cardiovascular disease.

"Overall, studies of meditation suggest a possible benefit on cardiovascular risk, although the overall quality and, in some cases, quantity of study data are modest. Given the low costs and low risks of this intervention, meditation may be considered as an adjunct to guideline-directed cardiovascular risk reduction by those interested in this lifestyle modification."

Does Mindfulness Meditation Improve Chronic Pain? A Systematic Review

Ball EF, et al. *Current Opinion in Obstetrics & Gynecology.* December 2017.

"Psychological factors are associated with chronic pain. Mindfulness meditation may ameliorate symptoms. The objective was to evaluate the effects of mindfulness meditation in chronic pain.

"A systematic search of four databases identified 534 citations; 13 Randomised controlled trials satisfied the inclusion criteria. Mindfulness meditation significantly reduced depression [Standardised mean difference (SMD) -0.28; 95% confidence interval (CI) -0.53, -0.03; P=0.03; I=0%]. For affective pain (SMD -0.13; 95% CI -0.42, 0.16; I=0%), sensory pain (SMD -0.02; 95% CI -0.31, 0.27; I=0%) and anxiety (SMD -0.16; 95% CI -0.47, 0.15; I=0%) there was a trend towards benefit with intervention. Quality of life items on mental health (SMD 0.65; 95% CI -0.27, 1.58; I=69%), physical health (SMD 0.08; 95% CI -0.40, 0.56; I=32%) and overall score (SMD 0.86, 95% CI -0.06, 1.78; I=88%) improved with mindfulness meditation.

"Mindfulness meditation has the most prominent effect on psychological aspects of living with chronic pain, improving associated depression and quality of life."

Relationships Between Mindfulness Practice and Levels of Mindfulness, Medical and Psychological Symptoms and Well-Being in a Mindfulness-Based Stress Reduction Program

Carmody J, Baer RA. *Journal of Behavioral Medicine.* February 2008.

"Relationships were investigated between home practice of mindfulness meditation exercises and levels of mindfulness, medical and psychological symptoms, perceived stress, and psychological well-being in a sample of 174 adults in a clinical Mindfulness-Based Stress Reduction (MBSR) program. This is an 8- session group program for individuals dealing with stress-related problems, illness, anxiety, and chronic pain. Participants completed measures of mindfulness, perceived stress, symptoms, and well-being at pre- and post-MBSR, and monitored their home practice time throughout the intervention. Results showed increases in mindfulness and well-being, and decreases in stress and symptoms, from pre- to post-MBSR. Time spent engaging in home practice of formal meditation exercises (body scan, yoga, sitting meditation) was significantly related to extent of improvement in most facets of mindfulness and several measures of symptoms and well-being."

Mindfulness Meditation for the Treatment of Chronic Low Back Pain in Older Adults: A Randomized Controlled Pilot Study

Morone NE, et al. *Pain*. February 2008.

"The objectives of this pilot study were to assess the feasibility of recruitment and adherence to an eight-session mindfulness meditation program for community-dwelling older adults with chronic low back pain (CLBP) and to develop initial estimates of treatment effects. It was designed as a randomized, controlled clinical trial. Participants were 37 community-dwelling older adults aged 65 years and older with CLBP of moderate intensity occurring daily or almost every day. Participants were randomized to an 8-week mindfulness-based meditation program or to a wait-list control group. Baseline, 8-week and 3-month follow-up measures of pain, physical function, and quality of life were assessed. Eighty-nine older adults were screened and 37 found to be eligible and randomized within a 6-month period. The mean age of the sample was 74.9 years, 21/37 (57%) of participants were female and 33/37 (89%) were white. At the end of the intervention 30/37 (81%) participants completed 8-week assessments. Average class attendance of the intervention arm was 6.7 out of 8. They meditated an average of 4.3 days a week and the average minutes per day was 31.6. Compared to the control group, the intervention group displayed significant improvement in the Chronic Pain Acceptance Questionnaire Total Score and Activities Engagement subscale (P=.008, P=.004) and SF-36 Physical Function (P=.03). The program may lead to improvement in pain acceptance and physical function."

Effect of Mindfulness Based Stress Reduction on Immune Function, Quality of Life and Coping in Women Newly Diagnosed with Early Stage Breast Cancer

Witek-Janusek L, et al. Brain Behavior & Immunity. March 20, 2008.

"This investigation used a non-randomized controlled design to evaluate the effect and feasibility of a mindfulness based stress reduction (MBSR) program on immune function, quality of life

(QOL), and coping in women recently diagnosed with breast cancer. Early stage breast cancer patients, who did not receive chemotherapy, self-selected into an 8-week MBSR program or into an assessment only, control group. Outcomes were evaluated over time. The first assessment was at least 10 days after surgery and prior to adjuvant therapy, as well as before the MBSR start-up. Further assessments were mid-MBSR, at completion of MBSR, and at 4-week post-MBSR completion. Women with breast cancer enrolled in the control group (Non-MBSR) were assessed at similar times. At the first assessment (i.e., before MBSR start), reductions in peripheral blood mononuclear cell NK cell activity (NKCA) and IFN-gamma production with increases in IL-4, IL-6, and IL-10 production and plasma cortisol levels were observed for both the MBSR and Non-MBSR groups of breast cancer patients. Over time women in the MBSR group re-established their NKCA and cytokine production levels. In contrast, breast cancer patients in the Non-MBSR group exhibited continued reductions in NKCA and IFN-gamma production with increased IL-4, IL-6, and IL-10 production. Moreover, women enrolled in the MBSR program had reduced cortisol levels, improved QOL, and increased coping effectiveness compared to the Non-MBSR group. In summary, MBSR is a program that is feasible for women recently diagnosed with early stage breast cancer and the results provide preliminary evidence for beneficial effects of MBSR; on immune function, QOL, and coping."

Mindfulness Training as an Intervention for Fibromyalgia: Evidence of Postintervention and 3-Year Follow-Up Benefits in Well-Being

Grossman P, et al. Psychotherapy and Psychosomatics. 2007.

"Mindfulness-based stress reduction (MBSR) proposes a systematic program for reduction of suffering associated with a wide range of medical conditions. Studies suggest improvements in general aspects of well-being, including quality of life (QoL), coping and positive affect, as well as decreased anxiety and depression. A quasi-experimental study examined the effects of an 8-week MBSR intervention among 58 female patients with fibromyalgia (mean, 52 +/- 8 years) who underwent MBSR or an active social support procedure. Participants were assigned to groups by date of entry, and 6 subjects dropped out during the study. Self-report measures were validated German inventories and included the following scales: visual analog pain, pain perception, coping with pain, a symptom checklist and QoL. Pre- and post intervention measurements were made. Additionally, a 3-year follow-up was carried out on a subgroup of 26 participants. RESULTS: Pre- to post intervention analyses indicated MBSR to provide significantly greater benefits than the control intervention on most dimensions, including visual analog pain, QoL subscales, coping with pain, anxiety, depression and somatic complaints (Cohen d effect size, 0.40-1.10). Three-year follow-up analyses of MBSR participants indicated sustained benefits for these same measures (effect size, 0.50-0.65). Based upon a quasi-randomized trial and long-term observational follow-up, results indicate mindfulness intervention to be of potential long-term benefit for female fibromyalgia patients."

A Longitudinal Study of Students' Perceptions of Using Deep Breathing Meditation to Reduce Testing Stresses.

Paul G, Elam B, Verhulst SJ. *Teach Learn Medicine*. Summer 2007.

"Stress can affect student performance. Yet few medical schools provide students with a consistent opportunity to develop and regularly practice stress reduction techniques to aid them academically. A curriculum component designed to assist 64 post-baccalaureate minority students in developing and practicing a stress-management technique was implemented on a regular basis from June 2004 to April 2006. Students participated in Deep Breathing Meditation exercises in two classes and completed pre-, post-, and follow-up surveys each academic year. Students reported having perceptions of decreased test anxiety, nervousness, self-doubt, and concentration loss, using the technique outside of the two classes, and believing it helped them academically and would help them as a physician. CONCLUSIONS: The Deep Breathing

Meditation technique was successfully implemented each academic year, and it provided students with a promising solution for meeting challenging academic and professional situations."

Systematic Review of the Efficacy of Meditation Techniques as Treatments for Medical Illness

Arias AJ, et al. *Journal of Alternative and Complementary Medicine.* October 2006.

"Meditative techniques are sought frequently by patients coping with medical and psychological problems. Because of their increasingly widespread appeal and use, and the potential for use as medical therapies, a concise and thorough review of the current state of scientific knowledge of these practices as medical interventions was conducted.

"Studies on normal healthy populations are not included. Searches were performed using PubMed, PsycInfo, and the Cochrane Database. Keywords were Meditation, Meditative Prayer, Yoga, Relaxation Response. Qualifying studies were reviewed and independently rated based on quality by two reviewers. Mid-to-high-quality studies (those scoring above 0.65 or 65% on a validated research quality scale) were included. RESULTS: From a total of 82 identified studies, 20 randomized controlled trials met our criteria. The studies included 958 subjects total (397 experimentally treated, 561 controls). No serious adverse events were reported in any of the included or excluded clinical trials. The strongest evidence for efficacy was found for epilepsy, symptoms of premenstrual syndrome and menopausal symptoms. Benefit was also demonstrated for mood and anxiety disorders, autoimmune illnesses, and emotional disturbance in neoplastic disease."

Effect of Rhythmic Breathing (Sudarshan Kriya and Pranayam) on Immune Functions and Tobacco Addiction

Kochupillai V. *Annals of New York Academy of Sciences.* November 2005.

"Stress, a psychophysiological process, acts through the immune-neuroendocrine axis and affects cellular processes of body and immune functions, leading to disease states, including cancer. Stress is also linked to the habit of tobacco consumption and substance abuse, which in turn also leads to diseases. Sudarshan Kriya (SK) and Pranayam (P), rhythmic breathing processes, are known to reduce stress and improve immune functions.

"Cancer patients who had completed their standard therapy were studied. SK and P increased natural killer (NK) cells significantly ($P < 0.001$) at 12 and 24 weeks of the practice compared to baseline. Increase in NK cells at 24 weeks was significant ($P < 0.05$) compared to controls. There was no effect on T-cell subsets after SK and P either in the study group or among controls. SK and P helped to control the tobacco habit in 21% of individuals who were followed up to 6 months of practice. We conclude that the inexpensive and easy to learn and practice breathing processes (SK and P) in this study demonstrated an increase in NK cells and a reduction in tobacco consumption. When confirmed in large and randomized studies, this result could mean that the regular practice of SK and P might reduce the incidence and progression of cancer."

BENEFITS OF POSITIVE THINKING

You know the ideas behind positive thinking have gotten deeply entrenched in mainstream culture when a conventional medical institution like the Mayo Clinic (www.mayoclinic.org) features this research and related advice on its website, in an article called "Positive Thinking: Stop Negative Self-Talk to Reduce Stress":

> "The positive thinking that usually comes with optimism is a key part of effective stress management," writes the Mayo Clinic medical staff. "Positive thinking often starts with self-talk. Self-talk is the endless stream of unspoken thoughts that run through your head. These automatic thoughts can be positive or negative. Some of your self-talk comes from logic and reason. Other self-talk may arise from misconceptions that you create because of lack of information. If the thoughts that run through your head are mostly negative, your outlook on life is more likely pessimistic. If your thoughts are mostly positive, you're likely an optimist—someone who practices positive thinking."

To cultivate positive thinking, scientists with Mayo recommend that (1) periodically, during the day, check in with what you're thinking and if your thoughts are mainly negative, concentrate on putting a positive spin on them; (2) daily exercise enhances mood, manages stress, and can keep thoughts positive; (3) keep yourself surrounded by positive people who know the value of humor and optimism; (4) engage in positive self-talk by never saying anything negative to yourself that you wouldn't verbally say to anyone else; (5) Think as often as possible about what you feel gratitude for in your life.

Positive Psychology, founded by the American psychologist Martin Seligman, in 2004, is a field of study that examines what gives our lives meaning and purpose in order to cultivate more optimism and positive thinking.

Does success bring about a positive attitude and happiness, or does happiness and a positive attitude to cultivate success? This chicken-or-egg question became the focus of a study in the journal *Psychological Bulletin* (Diener, et al., 2005), in which university psychologists reviewed the scientific literature and concluded: "Happy people—those who experience a preponderance of positive emotions—tend to be successful and accomplished across multiple life domains. Why is happiness linked to successful outcomes? We propose that this is not merely because success leads to happiness, but because positive affect (relating to life with positive thinking) engenders success. Positively valenced moods and emotions lead people to think, feel, and act in ways that promote both resource building and involvement with approach goals."

These findings were confirmed by a study in the *Journal of Career Assessment* (Boehm, et al., February 2008) in which social scientists found that "happiness is a source of why particular employees are more successful than others. . . . [H]appiness often precedes measures of success and induction of positive affect leads to improved workplace outcomes . . . and compared with their less happy peers, happy people earn more money, display superior performance, and perform more helpful acts."

A study published in the *American Journal of Epidemiology* (Kim, et al., January 2017), examining health data from more than 100,000 persons, even found "growing evidence {linking} positive psychological attributes like optimism to a lower risk of poor health outcomes, especially cardiovascular disease."

Here are more research examples of the importance of positive thinking on life and health and wealth outcomes:

Effects of the Maytiv Positive Psychology School Program on Early Adolescents' Well-Being, Engagement, and Achievement

Shoshani A, et al. *Journal of School Psychology*. August 2016.

"As positive psychology is a nascent area of research, there are very few empirical studies assessing the impact and sustained effects of positive psychology school interventions. The current study presents a 2-year longitudinal evaluation of the effects of a school-based positive psychology program on students' subjective well-being, school engagement, and academic achievements. The study investigated the effectiveness of the Maytiv school program using a positive psychology–based classroom-level intervention with 2517 seventh- to ninth-grade students in 70 classrooms, from six schools in the center of Israel.

"The classes were randomly assigned to intervention and control conditions, which were comparable in terms of students' age, gender, and socio-economic status. Hierarchical linear regression analyses revealed positive intervention effects on positive emotions, peer relations, emotional engagement in school, cognitive engagement, and grade point average scores (Cohen's ds 0.16-0.71). In the control group, there were significant decreases in positive emotions and cognitive engagement, and no significant changes in peer relations, emotional engagement or school achievements. These findings demonstrate the significant socio-emotional and academic benefits of incorporating components of positive psychology into school curricula."

The Power of Positive Thinking: Pathological Worry Is Reduced by Thought Replacement in Generalized Anxiety Disorder

Hirsch R, et al. Behaviour Research and Therapy. March 2016.

"Worry in Generalized Anxiety Disorder (GAD) takes a predominantly verbal form, as if talking to oneself about possible negative outcomes. The current study examined alternative approaches to reducing worry by allocating volunteers with GAD to conditions in which they either practiced replacing the usual form of worry with images of possible positive outcomes, or with the same positive outcomes represented verbally. A comparison control condition involved generating positive images not related to worries.

"Participants received training in the designated method and then practiced it for one week, before attending for reassessment, and completing follow-up questionnaires four weeks later. All groups benefited from training, with decreases in anxiety and worry, and no significant differences between groups. The replacement of worry with different forms of positive ideation, even when unrelated to the content of worry itself, seems to have similar beneficial effects, suggesting that any form of positive ideation can be used to effectively counter worry."

The Effect of Loving-Kindness Meditation on Positive Emotions: A Meta-Analytic Review

Zeng X, et al. *Frontiers in Psychology.* November 3, 2015.

"While it has been suggested that loving-kindness meditation (LKM) is an effective practice for promoting positive emotions, the empirical evidence in the literature remains unclear. Here, we provide a systematic review of 24 empirical studies (N = 1759) on LKM with self-reported positive emotions. The effect of LKM on positive emotions was estimated with meta-analysis, and the influence of variations across LKM interventions was further explored with subgroup analysis and meta-regression.

"The meta-analysis showed that (1) medium effect sizes for LKM interventions on daily positive emotions in both wait-list controlled RCTs and non-RCT studies; and (2) small to large effect sizes for the on-going practice of LKM on immediate positive emotions across different comparisons. Further analysis showed that (1) interventions focused on loving-kindness had medium effect size, but interventions focused on compassion showed small effect sizes; (2) the length of interventions and the time spent on meditation did not influence the effect sizes, but the studies without didactic components in interventions had small effect sizes. A few individual studies reported that the nature of positive emotions and individual differences also influenced the results.

"In sum, LKM practice and interventions are effective in enhancing positive emotions."

Loving-Kindness Meditation and the Broaden-and-Build Theory of Positive Emotions Among Veterans with Posttraumatic Stress Disorder

Kearney DJ, et al. *Medical Care.* December 2014.

"Loving-kindness meditation (LKM) is a practice intended to enhance feelings of kindness and compassion for self and others. To assess whether participation in a 12-week course of LKM for veterans with posttraumatic stress disorder (PTSD) is associated with improved positive emotions, decentering, and personal resources:

"A total of 42 veterans with active PTSD (40% female) participated. Emotions, decentering, psychological wellbeing including autonomy, environmental mastery, personal growth, positive relations, purpose in life, self-acceptance, and sense of social support were measured at each time point.

"Significant increases in unactivated pleasant (d=0.73), but not activated pleasant, emotions were found over time. Activated and unactivated unpleasant emotions decreased over time (d=-0.69 and -0.53, respectively). There were also increases in environmental mastery (d=0.61), personal growth (d=0.54), purpose in life (d=0.71), self-acceptance (d=0.68), and decentering (d=0.96) at 3-month follow-up. Overall, positive emotions increased, and enhancement of personal resources occurred over time."

Efficacy of Rajayoga Meditation on Positive Thinking: An Index for Self-Satisfaction and Happiness in Life

M G R, et al. *Journal of Clinical & Diagnostic Research.* October 2013.

"Psychological studies have shown that brief period of mindfulness meditation significantly improves critical cognitive skills. But, there are no studies which have assessed the effects of Brahma Kumaris Raja Yoga Meditation (BKRM) practice on positive thinking and happiness in life. The present study was designed to test the hypothesis is BKRM enhances positive thinking and that essential to attain higher levels of self-satisfaction and happiness in life.

"This study is a cross sectional comparative study which was done between Rajayoga meditators and non-meditators. This study was conducted at BKRM Centres at Manipal and Udupi in Karnataka, India. Fifty subjects were selected for this study, which included those practising BKRM in their normal routine life (n=25) and non-meditators (n=25) who were aged 42.95+/15.29 years. Self-reported Oxford happiness questionnaire (OHQ) was administered to all subjects and their happiness scores and status were assessed and compared.

"Mean happiness scores of BKRM were significantly higher (p<0.001) in meditators as compared to those in non-meditators. The number of meditators experiencing happiness status were significantly higher (p<0.05) in comparison with non-meditators. Additionally, meditators scored significantly higher on self-satisfaction items (p<0.001) as compared to non-meditators. BKRM helps in significantly increasing self-satisfaction and happiness in life by enhancing positive thinking. Irrespective of age and years of short-term or long-term meditation practice, enhanced positive thinking increases self-satisfaction and happiness in life."

Upward Spirals of Positive Emotions Counter Downward Spirals of Negativity: Insights from the Broaden-and-Build Theory and Affective Neuroscience on the Treatment of Emotion Dysfunctions and Deficits in Psychopathology

Garland EL, et al. *Clinical Psychology Review.* November 2010.

"This review integrates broaden-and-build theory of positive emotions with advances in affective neuroscience regarding plasticity in the neural circuitry of emotions to inform the treatment of emotion deficits within psychopathology. We first present a body of research showing that positive emotions broaden cognition and behavioral repertoires, and in so doing, build durable biopsychosocial resources that support coping and flourishing mental health.

"Next, by explicating the processes through which momentary experiences of emotions may accrue into self-perpetuating emotional systems, the current review proposes an underlying architecture of state-trait interactions that engenders lasting affective dispositions. This theoretical framework is then used to elucidate the cognitive-emotional mechanisms underpinning three disorders of affect regulation: depression, anxiety, and schizophrenia. In turn, two mind training interventions, mindfulness and loving-kindness meditation, are highlighted as means of generating positive emotions that may counter the negative affective processes implicated in these disorders. We conclude with the proposition that positive emotions may exert a countervailing force on the dysphoric, fearful, or anhedonic states characteristic of psychopathologies typified by emotional dysfunctions."

Open Hearts Build Lives: Positive Emotions, Induced Through Loving-Kindness Meditation, Build Consequential Personal Resources

Fredrickson BL, et al. *Journal of Personality & Social Psychology.* November 2008.

"B. L. Fredrickson's (1998, 2001) broaden-and-build theory of positive emotions asserts that people's daily experiences of positive emotions compound over time to build a variety of consequential personal resources. The authors tested this build hypothesis in a field experiment with working adults (n = 139), half of whom were randomly-assigned to begin the practice of loving-kindness meditation.

"Results showed that this meditation practice produced increases over time in daily experiences of positive emotions, which, in turn, produced increases in a wide range of personal resources (e.g., increased mindfulness, purpose in life, social support, decreased illness symptoms). In turn, these increments in personal resources predicted increased life satisfaction and reduced depressive symptoms."

Psychological Functioning and Physical Health: A Paradigm of Flexibility

Rozanski A, Kubzansky LD. *Psychosomatic Medicine.* May–June 2005.

"Recent evidence suggests that positive psychological factors may be protective against coronary artery disease (CAD). We consider this possibility through a paradigm that explores three inter-related factors that may promote healthy psychological functioning: vitality, emotional flexibility, and coping flexibility. Vitality is a positive and restorative emotional state that is associated with a sense of enthusiasm and energy. Flexibility is related both to the ability to regulate emotions effectively and cope effectively with challenging daily experiences. A variety of factors may diminish vitality, including chronic stress and negative emotions.

"Pathophysiologically, chronic stress and negative emotional states can both invoke a 'chronic stress response' characterized by increased stimulation of the sympathetic nervous system and hypothalamic-pituitary-adrenal axis, with resultant peripheral effects, including augmented heart rate and blood pressure responsiveness and delayed recovery to stressful stimuli. Research indicates a wide array of stressful conditions—associated with either elements of relative inflexibility in psychological functioning and/or relatively unabated stressful stimulation—that are associated with this type of exhausting hyperarousal.

"Conversely, new data suggest that positive psychological factors, including positive emotions, optimism, and social support, may diminish physiological hyperresponsiveness and/or reduce adverse clinical event rates. Still other positive factors such as gratitude and altruistic behavior have been linked to a heightened sense of well-being but have not yet been tested for beneficial physiological effects. Pending further study, these observations could serve as the basis for expanding the potential behavioral interventions that may be used to assist patients with psychosocial risk factors for CAD."

THE BENEFITS OF FORGIVENESS: TAKING RESPONSIBILITY, LETTING GO, FINDING SERENITY

Forgiving someone should be done for *your* sake, for *your* emotional healing, not to benefit the person who hurt you. By holding grudges and coddling resentments, you create real health consequences for yourself. So think of forgiveness as the choice you make to take responsibility for how *you* feel. It's a choice to experience a healing peace of mind, and with it the ability to remove emotional barriers that undermine wellness.

"You have an unresolved grievance. You blame the person who hurt you for how bad you feel. Forgiveness is the peace you feel when you resolve that grievance," observes Fred Luskin, PhD, the cofounder and director of the Stanford University Forgiveness Project and author of *Forgive for Good: A Proven Prescription for Health and Happiness.*

"Forgiveness can be taught and learned, just like learning to throw a baseball," Dr. Luskin assures us.

If you're interested in a long and healthy life, you should definitely enroll in Forgiveness 101. Medical studies show that people who blame others for their troubles have a higher incidence of heart disease and cancer. Studies also show that people who are forgiving have fewer health problems overall, including fewer physical symptoms from stress. "Every time you revisit a sense of grievance, you cause stress to the body," says Luskin.

To give you an example, in a study where people imagined either forgiving or not forgiving someone, those imagining forgiveness had increased blood flow, less muscle tension and lower levels of stress hormones—while those not imagining forgiveness experienced negative changes in all those measurements.

Luskin cautions us to remember that forgiveness is not about being a doormat for injustice. "Forgiveness doesn't mean condoning unkindness, forgetting that something painful happened, excusing poor behavior, or reconciling with the offender. Forgiveness is a skill that frees you from unnecessary emotional pain and poor health."

Tuning In to the Forgiveness Channel

If you can imagine your mind as being akin to a television, Luskin encourages you to learn how you can "change the channel" from grievance to forgiveness: "When you bring more positive experiences into your life, your hurts [and your perceived wrongs] will diminish."

To tune in to the Forgiveness Channel, he recommends:

- Look for examples of people in your life who have successfully forgiven other people who have hurt them. Ask them to relate their stories and describe how they did it. You may be motivated to follow the same path.

- Get inspiration from people you don't personally know who have gotten past hurtful and traumatic incidents or circumstances. You might try reading books like: A Man Named Dave: A Story of Triumph and Forgiveness (about a man who suffered child abuse and subsequently forgave his father).,

- Have you already forgiven someone in your life? Try to remember examples of who, what, where, and when. How did you feel afterward?

- Remind yourself of those times when you may have hurt others and needed to feel their forgiveness. Remember how you reacted when they forgave you? Did that feeling inspire you to do anything positive in return?

- Practice forgiving the little offenses we experience in life, like a careless driver who cuts you off in traffic. Or practice forgiving a friend who didn't call or arrive when she or he said they would. Or you can practice noticing when someone is kind to you even after you've been rude or hurtful.

Practice This "Positive Emotion Refocusing Technique"

Maintaining serenity in any situation—no matter how disturbing it feels—is a necessary state of being for forgiveness to happen, Luskin writes. He has developed a technique called PERT: Positive Emotion Refocusing Technique, to help counteract the effects of an unresolved grievance or ongoing relationship problem.

It consists of two steps:

1. Bring your attention fully to your abdomen and inhale deeply one or two times. As you inhale, gentle push your belly out. As you exhale, consciously relax and "soften" your belly.

2. Take a deep breath and imagine someone you love, or a beautiful scene in nature that fills you with awe. While continuing with your abdominal breathing, ask the serene part of you what you can do to resolve the difficulty you feel.

Luskin writes that the "daily practice of PERT can give you the power to see that focusing on your grievances hurts you more than the offender." Through PERT, you can regain and manage power over your emotions.

Forgiveness has been studied extensively by scientists, especially how a practice of forgiveness can help to treat alcoholism, anxiety, cardiovascular disease, depression, drug addiction, high blood pressure, pain, and stress.

Meta-Analytic Connections Between Forgiveness and Health: The Moderating Effects of Forgiveness-Related Distinctions

Rasmussen KR, et al. *Psychology & Health.* January 11, 2009.

"We explore meta-analytic associations between health and forgiveness, testing a number of potential theoretical and methodological factors that could alter that association, including the type of forgiveness measure (e.g. state vs. trait), the type of health measure (i.e. physical vs. psychological) and the target of forgiveness (e.g. self- vs. other-forgiveness).

"Our findings below reflect the meta-analysis of 103 independent samples consisting of 606 correlations with a total sample of 26,043 participants. The final sample included papers from 17 countries. The included samples were diverse including students, older adults, divorced mothers, combat veterans and others.

"Various health measures, including physical health outcomes (e.g., blood pressure, cortisol levels, bodily pain) and psychological health outcomes (e.g., depression, anxiety, PTSD). We found a reliable overall association between forgiveness and health outcomes. The association was stronger for psychological health than for physical health, though associations with cardiovascular health indicators (i.e. heart-rate and blood pressure) were robust."

Traditional Bullying, Cyberbullying and Mental Health in Early Adolescents: Forgiveness as a Protective Factor of Peer Victimisation

Quintana-Orts C, Rey L. *International Journal of Environmental Research and Public Health.* October 28, 2018.

"Traditional and online bullying are prevalent throughout adolescence. Given their negative consequences, it is necessary to seek protective factors to reduce or even prevent their detrimental effects on the mental health of adolescents before they become chronic. Previous studies have demonstrated the protective role of forgiveness in mental health after several transgressions.

"This study assessed whether forgiveness moderated the effects of bullying victimisation and cyber victimization on mental health in a sample of 1044 early adolescents (527 females; $M=$ 13.09 years; $SD = 0.77$). Participants completed a questionnaire battery that measures both forms of bullying victimisation, suicidal thoughts and behaviours, satisfaction with life, and forgiveness.

"Consistent with a growing body of research, results reveal that forgiveness is a protective factor against the detrimental effects of both forms of bullying. Among more victimised and cyber victimised adolescents, those with high levels of forgiveness were found to report significantly higher levels of satisfaction compared to those with low levels of forgiveness. Likewise, those reporting traditional victimisation and higher levels of forgiveness levels showed lower levels of suicidal risk. Our findings contribute to an emerging relationship between forgiveness after bullying and indicators of mental health, providing new areas for research and intervention."

Hostility, Forgiveness, and Cognitive Impairment over 10 Years in a National Sample of American Adults

Toussaint LL, et al. *Health Psychology*. December 2018.

"We examined the extent to which self-forgiveness and forgiveness of others moderated the association of hostility with changes in cognitive impairment over 10 years in a nationally representative sample of adults in the United States.

"Participants were 1,084 respondents to the Americans' Changing Lives survey, a longitudinal study of American adults. Hostility, self-forgiveness, forgiveness of others, and cognitive impairment were measured at baseline, and cognitive impairment was assessed again at follow-up. Moderated multiple regression analyses tested whether self-forgiveness and forgiveness of others moderated the association of hostility with changes in cognitive impairment over time, controlling for baseline cognitive impairment and relevant sociodemographic and clinical factors.

"As hypothesized, greater hostility levels at baseline predicted more cognitive impairment 10 years later, $\beta = .08$, $p < .01$. In addition, self-forgiveness at baseline moderated the association between baseline hostility and cognitive impairment at follow-up, $\beta = -.07$, $p < .01$. Decomposing this interaction revealed that hostility significantly predicted increased cognitive impairment at follow-up for individuals with low, $\beta = .15$, $p < .001$, and average, $\beta = .08$, $p = .001$, levels of self-forgiveness but not for persons with high levels of self-forgiveness, $\beta = .03$, $p = .34$. In contrast, forgiveness of others was not a significant moderator.

"CONCLUSIONS: Greater hostility is associated with the development of more cognitive impairment over 10 years, and being more self-forgiving appears to mitigate these hostility-related effects on cognition. Enhancing self-forgiveness may thus represent one possible strategy for promoting cognitive resilience in adulthood."

Childhood Victimization, Recent Injustice, Anger, and Forgiveness in a Sample of Imprisoned Male Offenders

Erzar T, et al. *International Journal of Offender Therapy and Comparative Criminology.* January 2019.

"The links between childhood victimization, subsequent emotional dysregulation, and insufficient coping skills have been repeatedly documented in the scientific literature. However, there is a gap in the literature regarding the role of forgiveness as a coping strategy and relationships between offense-specific hurt, chronic anger, and early victimization. The goals of our study were (a) to explore how offenders cope with recent unjust treatment, and test the links between type of injustice, hurt experienced due to injustice, and use of forgiveness; (b) to test the links between childhood victimization, hurt, and chronic anger; and (c) to assess the mediating role of chronic anger in relation to hurt and forgiveness.

"The results reveal that multiplicity and severity of victimization exposure in the prison sample are positively associated with chronic anger, but not with hurt. The type of injustice affects the level of hurt and forgiveness, while chronic anger mediates the link between hurt and forgiveness. To improve coping and promote forgiving, offenders should be helped to identify everyday sources of stress and learn to express vulnerable feelings beneath anger."

Longitudinal Relationship Between Forgiveness of Self and Forgiveness of Others Among Individuals with Alcohol Use Disorders

Krentzman AR, et al. *Psychology of Religion and Spirituality*. May 2018.

"Previous research has suggested that forgiveness of self and forgiveness of others might function differently over the course of addiction recovery. However, we know little about the longitudinal process of these dimensions of forgiveness for individuals addressing alcohol-use disorders. Increased knowledge would inform the content and sequencing of intervention strategies.

"Three hundred and sixty-four individuals managing alcohol dependence participated in a 30-month longitudinal study, reporting their capacity to forgive self and to forgive others every 6 months. Findings indicated that a) participants were more forgiving of others than themselves, b) both types of forgiveness increased over time, c) forgiveness of self increased more rapidly than forgiveness of others, and d) while increases in both types of forgiveness predicted increases in the other type, the effect of forgiveness of others on forgiveness of self was twice as strong as the reverse effect."

"You're Forgiven, but Don't Do It Again!" Direct Partner Regulation Buffers the Costs of Forgiveness

Russell VM, et al. Journal of Family Psychology. June 2018.

"Although forgiveness can have numerous benefits, it can also have a notable cost—forgiveness can allow transgressors to continue behaving in ways that can be hurtful (McNulty, 2010, 2011). Accordingly, two studies tested the prediction that the implications of forgiveness for whether the partner transgresses or fails to behave benevolently depend on whether forgivers regulate partners away from future transgressions and toward benevolent behaviors.

"Study 1 was an experimental study of emerging adult couples in which participants were (a) asked to report their partners' tendencies to engage in partner-regulation behaviors, (b) led to believe their partners were either forgiving or unforgiving, and (c) given the opportunity to transgress against their partners. Study 2 was a longitudinal study of newlywed couples in which participants were (a) asked to report their tendencies to forgive their partners, (b) observed during problem-solving discussions, and then (c) asked to report their satisfaction with their partners' considerateness every 6 months for 4 years.

"Both studies provided evidence that direct oppositional partner-regulation behaviors moderate the implications of forgiveness for partner behavior. Among intimates who demanded more change, forgiveness was associated with the partner transgressing less (Study 1) and compromising more (Study 2), as well as participants being more satisfied with their partners' considerateness over time (Study 2); among intimates who demanded less change, forgiveness was associated with these outcomes in the opposite direction. These findings suggest that supplementing forgiveness with partner-regulation behaviors can help non distressed couples avoid the undesirable outcomes and maximize desirable outcomes associated with forgiveness."

Associations Between Women's Experiences of Sexual Violence and Forgiveness

Davidson MM, et al. *Violence and Victims.* 2013.

"The purpose of this study was to examine forgiveness and sexual violence among college women. Undergraduate women (N = 503) completed an online survey assessing experiences of sexual violence and forgiveness. Simultaneous multivariate regressions revealed that experiencing more sexual violence was associated with more revenge and avoidance, and less benevolence.

"Furthermore, findings indicated that more experiences of sexual violence were negatively associated with forgiveness of self, forgiveness of others, and forgiveness of uncontrollable situations. This work begins to fill critical gaps in the extant literature because it is the only study to date that examines sexual violence and the positive psychological construct of forgiveness."

Unforgiveness, Depression, and Health in Later Life: The Protective Factor of Forgivingness

Ermer AE, Proulx CM. *Aging & Mental Health.* October 2016.

"Feeling unforgiven by others has been linked to poor health outcomes. The current study examined whether feeling unforgiven by others is associated with depression and self-rated health among older adults in the United States. The potential moderating roles of forgiving others and self-forgiveness in the association between unforgiveness and both depression and self-rated health was also assessed along with gender differences.

"Data were drawn from a sample of 1009 adults in Wave 2 of the Religion, Aging, and Health Survey, a national sample of adults aged over 67. Depression was measured using the eight item short form from the Center for Epidemiologic Studies-Depression (CES-D) scale. Self-rated health was assessed with a one-item indicator.

"Analyses indicated that higher levels of self-forgiveness ameliorated the relationship between unforgiveness by others and depression for men and women and higher levels of forgiving others attenuated the association between unforgiveness by others and depression for women. Self-forgiveness was protective of depression for women who reported unforgiveness by others and low levels of forgiving others. Regardless of levels of self-forgiveness, men who were most likely to forgive others experienced a significant association between unforgiveness by others and depression. Neither forgiving others nor the self were significant moderators in the association between unforgiveness and self-rated health. Forgiving others and the self may be protective of well-being when women feel unforgiven by others."

Writing About the Benefits of an Interpersonal Transgression Facilitates Forgiveness

McCullough ME, Root LM, Cohen AD. *Journal of Consulting Clinical Psychology.* October 2006.

"The authors examined the effects of writing about the benefits of an interpersonal transgression on forgiveness. Participants (N = 304) were randomly assigned to one of three 20-min writing tasks in which they wrote about either (a) traumatic features of the most recent interpersonal transgression they had suffered, (b) personal benefits resulting from the transgression, or (c) a control topic that was unrelated to the transgression.

"Participants in the benefit-finding condition became more forgiving toward their transgressors than did those in the other 2 conditions, who did not differ from each other. In part, the benefit-finding condition appeared to facilitate forgiveness by encouraging participants to engage in cognitive processing as they wrote their essays. Results suggest that benefit finding may be a unique and useful addition to efforts to help people forgive interpersonal transgressions through structured interventions."

Forgiveness and Chronic Low Back Pain: A Preliminary Study Examining the Relationship of Forgiveness to Pain, Anger, and Psychological Distress

Carson JW, et al. *Journal of Pain.* February 2005.

"Clinical observations suggest that many patients with chronic pain have difficulty forgiving persons they perceive as having unjustly offended them in some way. By using a sample of 61 patients with chronic low back pain, this study sought to determine the reliability and variability of forgiveness assessments in patients and to examine the relationship of forgiveness to pain, anger, and psychological distress.

"Standardized measures were used to assess patients' current levels of forgiveness, forgiveness self-efficacy, pain, anger, and psychological distress. Results showed that forgiveness-related constructs can be reliably assessed in patients with persistent pain, and that patients vary considerably along dimensions of forgiveness. Furthermore, correlational analyses showed that patients who had higher scores on forgiveness-related variables reported lower levels of pain, anger, and psychological distress.

"These findings indicate that forgiveness can be reliably assessed in patients with persistent pain, and that a relationship appears to exist between forgiveness and important aspects of living with persistent pain. This preliminary study suggests there is a relationship between forgiveness and pain, anger, and psychological distress in patients with chronic low back pain. Patients who report an inability to forgive others might be experiencing higher pain and psychological distress that are mediated by relatively higher levels of state anger."

BENEFITS OF GRATITUDE: HAVING AN ATTITUDE OF GRATITUDE— MORE THAN A CLICHÉ

Gratitude is having a feeling that you've received a benefit or gift, says Robert A. Emmons, PhD, a professor of psychology at the University of California in Davis. Dr. Emmons is a pioneering psychologist in studying how gratitude affects us emotionally and physically.

Dr. Emmons did a study in which he had a group of people write down what they were grateful for, while another group only wrote about what was going wrong in their lives. He did assessments after a few weeks and found that those in the "gratitude group" had more energy, more enthusiasm for life, and even slept better than those in the group voicing complaints.

"An attitude of gratitude—even in the midst of suffering—is going to have an effect on the health of the body and mind," Dr. Emmons writes. "Being grateful builds social relationships, and studies show that people with more social support are healthier than those without it."

Can you consciously *develop* an attitude of gratitude? The answer is yes, because gratitude is not a trait but a conscious choice, and gratitude is a feeling that can be cultivated.

Scientists have studied the impact of people's practice of expressing gratitude on improving the recovery from a range of conditions: alcoholism, anxiety, cancer, depression, high blood pressure, HIV/AIDS, and stress. Here are excerpts from some of these scientific studies.

Effects of Gratitude Meditation on Neural Network Functional Connectivity and Brain-Heart Coupling

Kyeong S, et al. *Scientific Reports.* July 1l, 2017.

"A sense of gratitude is a powerful and positive experience that can promote a happier life, whereas resentment is associated with life dissatisfaction. To explore the effects of gratitude and resentment on mental well-being, we acquired functional magnetic resonance imaging and heart rate (HR) data before, during, and after the gratitude and resentment interventions. Functional connectivity (FC) analysis was conducted to identify the modulatory effects of gratitude on the default mode, emotion, and reward-motivation networks.

"The average HR was significantly lower during the gratitude intervention than during the resentment intervention. Temporostriatal FC showed a positive correlation with HR during the gratitude intervention, but not during the resentment intervention. Temporostriatal resting-state FC was significantly decreased after the gratitude intervention compared to the resentment intervention. After the gratitude intervention, resting-state FC of the amygdala with the right dorsomedial prefrontal cortex and left dorsal anterior cingulate cortex were positively correlated with anxiety scale and depression scale, respectively. Taken together, our findings shed light on the effect of gratitude meditation on an individual's mental well-being, and indicate that it may be a means of improving both emotion regulation and self-motivation by modulating resting-state FC in emotion and motivation-related brain regions."

The Effects of Gratitude Expression on Neural Activity

Kini P, et al. *Neuroimage*. March 2016.

"Gratitude is a common aspect of social interaction, yet relatively little is known about the neural bases of gratitude expression, nor how gratitude expression may lead to longer-term effects on brain activity. To address these twin issues, we recruited subjects who coincidentally were entering psychotherapy for depression and/or anxiety.

"One group participated in a gratitude writing intervention, which required them to write letters expressing gratitude. The therapy-as-usual control group did not perform a writing intervention. After three months, subjects performed a 'Pay It Forward' task in the fMRI scanner. In the task, subjects were repeatedly endowed with a monetary gift and then asked to pass it on to a charitable cause to the extent they felt grateful for the gift. Operationalizing gratitude as monetary gifts allowed us to engage the subjects and quantify the gratitude expression for subsequent analyses. We measured brain activity and found regions where activity correlated with self-reported gratitude experience during the task, even including related constructs such as guilt motivation and desire to help as statistical controls. These were mostly distinct from brain regions activated by empathy or theory of mind.

"Also, our between groups cross-sectional study found that a simple gratitude writing intervention was associated with significantly greater and lasting neural sensitivity to gratitude—subjects who participated in gratitude letter writing showed both behavioral increases in gratitude and significantly greater neural modulation by gratitude in the medial prefrontal cortex three months later."

The Cultivation of Pure Altruism via Gratitude: A Functional MRI Study of Change with Gratitude Practice

Karns CM, et al. *Frontiers in Human Neuroscience.* December 12, 2017.

"Gratitude is an emotion and a trait linked to well-being and better health, and welcoming benefits to oneself is instrumentally valuable. However, theoretical and empirical work highlights that gratitude is more fully understood as an intrinsically valuable moral emotion. To understand the role of neural reward systems in the association between gratitude and altruistic motivations we tested two hypotheses: First, whether self-reported propensity toward gratitude relates to fMRI-derived indicators of 'pure altruism,' operationalized as the neural valuation of passive, private transfers to a charity versus to oneself.

"In young adult female participants, self-reported gratitude and altruism were associated with 'neural pure altruism' in ventromedial prefrontal cortex (VMPFC) and nucleus accumbens. Second, whether neural pure altruism can be increased through practicing gratitude. In a double-blind study, we randomly assigned participants to either a gratitude-journal or active-neutral control journal group for 3 weeks. Relative to pre-test levels, gratitude journaling increased the neural pure altruism response in the VMPFC. We posit that as a context-dependent value-sensitive cortical region, the VMPFC supports change with gratitude practice, a change that is larger for benefits to others versus oneself."

Neural Correlates of Gratitude

Fox GR, et al. *Frontiers of Psychology.* September 30, 2015.

"Gratitude is an important aspect of human sociality, and is valued by religions and moral philosophies. It has been established that gratitude leads to benefits for both mental health and interpersonal relationships. It is thus important to elucidate the neurobiological correlates of gratitude, which are only now beginning to be investigated. To this end, we conducted an experiment during which we induced gratitude in participants while they underwent functional magnetic resonance imaging.

"We hypothesized that gratitude ratings would correlate with activity in brain regions associated with moral cognition, value judgment and theory of mind. The stimuli used to elicit gratitude were drawn from stories of survivors of the Holocaust, as many survivors report being sheltered by strangers or receiving lifesaving food and clothing, and having strong feelings of gratitude for such gifts. The participants were asked to place themselves in the context of the Holocaust and imagine what their own experience would feel like if they received such gifts. For each gift, they rated how grateful they felt.

"The results revealed that ratings of gratitude correlated with brain activity in the anterior cingulate cortex and medial prefrontal cortex, in support of our hypotheses. The results provide a window into the brain circuitry for moral cognition and positive emotion that accompanies the experience of benefitting from the goodwill of others."

The Proximal Experience of Gratitude

Layous K, et al. *PLoS One.* July 7, 2017.

"Although a great deal of research has tested the longitudinal effects of regularly practicing gratitude, much less attention has been paid to the emotional landscape directly following engagement in gratitude exercises. In three studies, we explored the array of discrete emotions people experience after being prompted to express or recall gratitude. In Studies 1 and 2, two different gratitude exercises produced not only greater feelings of gratitude relative to two positive emotion control conditions (i.e., recalling relief), but also higher levels of other socially relevant states like elevation, connectedness, and indebtedness. In a third study, conducted in both the U.S. and S. Korea, we compared a gratitude exercise to another positive emotion elicitation (i.e., recalling a kind act) and to a neutral task, and again found that the gratitude exercise prompted greater gratitude, elevation, indebtedness, and guilt, but no more embarrassment or shame, than the two comparison conditions.

"Additionally, in all three studies, emodiversity and cluster analyses revealed that gratitude exercises led to the simultaneous experience of both pleasant and unpleasant socially-relevant states. In sum, although it may seem obvious that gratitude exercises would evoke grateful, positive states, a meta-analysis of our three studies revealed that gratitude exercises actually elicit a mixed emotional experience-one that simultaneously leads individuals to feel uplifted and indebted."

Does Gratitude Enhance Prosociality?
A Meta-Analytic Review

Ma LK, et al. *Psychological Bulletin.* June 2017.

"Theoretical models suggest that gratitude is linked to increased prosociality. To date, however, there is a lack of a comprehensive quantitative synthesis of results to support this claim. In this review we aimed to (a) examine the overall strength of the association between gratitude and prosociality, and (b) identify the theoretical and methodological variables that moderate this link. We identified 252 effect sizes from 91 studies across 65 papers-(Total N = 18,342 participants).

"The present meta-analysis revealed a statistically significant, and moderate positive correlation between gratitude and prosociality (r = .374). This association was significantly larger among studies that assessed *reciprocal* outcomes relative to *nonreciprocal* outcomes, and in particular among studies that examined *direct*-compared with *indirect*-reciprocity. Studies that examined gratitude as an *affective state* reported significantly larger effect size studies assessing gratitude as a *trait*. Studies that examined *benefit-triggered* gratitude (in response to others kindness) had a stronger effect that *generalized* gratitude that focuses on the appreciation of what is valued and cherished in life. Finally, studies that manipulated gratitude in vivo (e.g., economic games) had larger effect sizes compared with those based on recalled incidents when the person felt grateful."

Gratitude and Well-Being:
A Review and Theoretical Integration

Wood AM, et al. *Clinical Psychology Review.* November 2010.

"This paper presents a new model of gratitude incorporating not only the gratitude that arises following help from others but also a habitual focusing on and appreciating the positive aspects of life, incorporating not only the gratitude that arises following help from others, but also a habitual focusing on and appreciating the positive aspects of life.

"Research into individual differences in gratitude and well-being is reviewed, including gratitude and psychopathology, personality, relationships, health, subjective and eudaimonic well-being, and humanistically oriented functioning. Gratitude is strongly related to well-being, however defined, and this link may be unique and causal. Interventions to clinically increase gratitude are critically reviewed, and concluded to be promising, although the positive psychology literature may have neglected current limitations, and a distinct research strategy is suggested.

"Finally, mechanisms whereby gratitude may relate to well-being are discussed, including schematic biases, coping, positive affect, and broaden-and-build principles. Gratitude is relevant to clinical psychology due to (a) strong explanatory power in understanding well-being, and (b) the potential of improving well-being through fostering gratitude with simple exercises."

Gender Differences in Gratitude: Examining Appraisals, Narratives, the Willingness to Express Emotions, and Changes in Psychological Needs

Kashdan TB, et al. *Journal of Personality.* June 2009.

"Previous work suggests women might possess an advantage over men in experiencing and benefiting from gratitude. We examined whether women perceive and react to gratitude differently than men. In Study 1, women, compared with men, evaluated gratitude expression to be less complex, uncertain, conflicting, and more interesting and exciting. In Study 2, college students and older adults described and evaluated a recent episode when they received a gift. Women, compared with men, reported less burden and obligation and greater gratitude. Upon gift receipt, older men reported the least positive affect when their benefactors were men. In Studies 2 and 3, women endorsed higher trait gratitude compared with men. In Study 3, over 3 months, women with greater gratitude were more likely to satisfy needs to belong and feel autonomous; gratitude had the opposite effect in men. The willingness to openly express emotions partially mediated gender differences, and effects could not be attributed to global trait affect.

"Results demonstrated that men were less likely to feel and express gratitude, made more critical evaluations of gratitude, and derived fewer benefits. Implications for the study and therapeutic enhancement of gratitude are discussed."

Gratitude Influences Sleep Through the Mechanism of Pre-Sleep Cognitions

Wood AM, et al. *Journal of Psychosomatic Research*. January 2009.

"To test whether individual differences in gratitude are related to sleep after controlling for neuroticism and other traits. To test whether pre-sleep cognitions are the mechanism underlying this relationship. A cross-sectional questionnaire study was conducted with a large (186 males, 215 females) community sample (ages=18-68 years, mean=24.89, S.D.=9.02), including 161 people (40%) scoring above 5 on the Pittsburgh Sleep Quality Index, indicating clinically impaired sleep. Measures included gratitude, the Pittsburgh Sleep Quality Index (PSQI), self-statement test of pre-sleep cognitions, the Mini-IPIP scales of Big Five personality traits, and the Social Desirability Scale.

"Gratitude predicted greater subjective sleep quality and sleep duration, and less sleep latency and daytime dysfunction. The relationship between gratitude and each of the sleep variables was mediated by more positive pre-sleep cognitions and less negative pre-sleep cognitions. All of the results were independent of the effect of the Big Five personality traits (including neuroticism) and social desirability.

"This is the first study to show that a positive trait is related to good sleep quality above the effect of other personality traits, and to test whether pre-sleep cognitions are the mechanism underlying the relationship between any personality trait and sleep. The study is also the first to show that trait gratitude is related to sleep and to explain why this occurs, suggesting future directions for research, and novel clinical implications.